Christopher Reeve

Titles in the People in the News series include:

PEOPLE
IN THE NEWS

Christopher Reeve

by Walter Oleksy

Lucent Books, San Diego, CA

No part of this book may be reproduced or used in any form or by any means, electrical, mechanical, or otherwise, including, but not limited to, photocopy, recording, or any information storage and retrieval system, without prior written permission from the publisher.

Oleksy wishes to thank the writers quoted in his biography of Christopher Reeve, their publishers, and members of the Christopher Reeve Homepage on the Internet: Steven Younis, Judy Thomas, and Joyce Kavitsky who graciously shared their vast knowledge of Mr. Reeve.

Library of Congress Cataloging-in-Publication Data

Oleksy, Walter G., 1930–
  Christopher Reeve / by Walter Oleksy.
    p. cm. — (People in the news)
  Includes bibliographical references and index.
  Summary: Discusses the personal life, acting career, tragic accident, and determination to recover of the actor known for his role as Superman and for his efforts on behalf of spinal cord injury victims.
  ISBN 1-56006-534-6 (lib. bdg. : alk. paper)
  1. Reeve, Christopher, 1952–   Juvenile literature. 2. Motion picture actors and actresses—United States Biography Juvenile literature. [1. Reeve, Christopher, 1952–   . 2. Actors and actresses. 3. Quadriplegics. 4. Physically handicapped.]
I. Title. II. Series: People in the news (San Diego, Calif.)
PN2287.R292043   2000
791.43'028'092—dc21
[B]
                              99-29830
                                CIP

Table of Contents

Foreword

F AME AND CELEBRITY are alluring. People are drawn to those who walk in fame's spotlight, whether they are known for great accomplishments or for notorious deeds. The lives of the famous pique public interest and attract attention, perhaps because their experiences seem in some ways so different from, yet in other ways so similar to, our own.

Newspapers, magazines, and television regularly capitalize on this fascination with celebrity by running profiles of famous people. For example, television programs such as *Entertainment Tonight* devote all of their programming to stories about entertainment and entertainers. Magazines such as *People* fill their pages with stories of the private lives of famous people. Even newspapers, newsmagazines, and television news frequently delve into the lives of well-known personalities. Despite the number of articles and programs, few provide more than a superficial glimpse at their subjects.

Lucent's People in the News series offers young readers a deeper look into the lives of today's newsmakers, the influences that have shaped them, and the impact they have had in their fields of endeavor and on other people's lives. The subjects of the series hail from many disciplines and walks of life. They include authors, musicians, athletes, political leaders, entertainers, entrepreneurs, and others who have made a mark on modern life and who, in many cases, will continue to do so for years to come.

These biographies are more than factual chronicles. Each book emphasizes the contributions, accomplishments, or deeds that have brought fame or notoriety to the individual and shows how that person has influenced modern life. Authors portray their subjects in a realistic, unsentimental light. For example, Bill Gates—the cofounder and chief executive officer of the software giant Microsoft—has been instrumental in making personal computers the most vital tool of the modern age. Few dispute his business savvy, his perseverance, or his technical expertise, yet critics say he is ruthless in his dealings with competitors and driven more by his desire to maintain Microsoft's dominance in the computer industry than by an interest in furthering technology.

In these books, young readers will encounter inspiring stories about real people who achieved success despite enormous obstacles. Oprah Winfrey—the most powerful, most watched, and wealthiest woman on television today—spent the first six years of her life in the care of her grandparents while her unwed mother sought work and a better life elsewhere. Her adolescence was colored by promiscuity, pregnancy at age fourteen, rape, and sexual abuse.

Each author documents and supports his or her work with an array of primary and secondary source quotations taken from diaries, letters, speeches, and interviews. All quotes are footnoted to show readers exactly how and where biographers derive their information and provide guidance for further research. The quotations enliven the text by giving readers eyewitness views of the life and accomplishments of each person covered in the People in the News series.

In addition, each book in the series includes photographs, annotated bibliographies, timelines, and comprehensive indexes. For both the casual reader and the student researcher, the People in the News series offers insight into the lives of today's newsmakers—people who shape the way we live, work, and play in the modern age.

Introduction

Actor and Real-Life Hero

BARELY OUT OF COLLEGE, tall, handsome, athletic and super-active Christopher Reeve became world-famous seemingly overnight as the movies' Superman. To millions of people he was their stalwart comic book hero come to life on the screen. Even Reeve said he looked like Superman and that he got the part mostly for that reason.

Publicly invincible, Reeve was, however, privately vulnerable. His parents' divorce when he was only four years old had left him with a sense of not belonging to a family. His mother's remarriage when he was nine, and his own later first attempt at a serious relationship, had not fulfilled his hunger to be part of a family.

Reeve felt secure and happy in being part of the stage family of theater people, but what followed his movie success as Superman disappointed him. What he had feared in taking on the part of the caped crusader in tights had come to pass: He was identified too closely with the character of Superman. Critics and the public

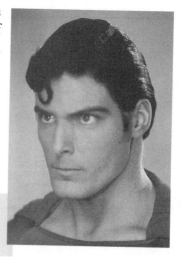

Reeve, shown here in his role as Superman, longed to be taken seriously as a versatile, professional actor.

tended not to accept him in any other role, even though Reeve saw himself as a versatile, professional actor.

While trying to change the public's image of him on the screen and the stage, and to bring more significance to his life, he turned social and political activist. He became an advocate for the environment, children's causes, AIDS victims and research, and preserving public funding for the arts. He even risked his life in Chile in defense of creative freedom.

At the height of his movie career and activism, and finally finding happiness in a family of his own, Reeve suffered a near-fatal horseback riding injury that left him a quadriplegic. People all over the world were shocked that the still-young man who personified Superman was now unable to walk or use his arms and could barely speak.

Refusing to let his devastating spinal cord injury end a meaningful life for him, Reeve has continued his career and activism from a wheelchair. While becoming a director and returning to acting, his main focus as an activist has become

At a Senate Labor subcommittee hearing on Capitol Hill in June 1997, Reeve lobbies from his wheelchair for an increase in federal funding for spinal cord injury research.

lobbying to raise insurance caps for paralysis victims and encouraging more government funding for spinal cord injury research.

As a leader in the family of the paralyzed, Reeve says he has become president of a club he would never have wanted to join. Because of his courage not to give up despite his disability, he has won the respect and admiration of millions. He is still Superman, even as he sits in a wheelchair and speaks with the aid of a ventilator—on behalf of tens of thousands of other paralysis victims like himself.

Because of his advocacy for spinal cord injury victims and his courage despite adversity, Reeve has become a real-life hero. This is his remarkable and inspirational story.

Chapter 1

A Boy in Search of a Family

CHRISTOPHER REEVE'S CHILDHOOD was marred by divorce and the absence of a feeling of closeness to either of his parents. His natural response was to withdraw from those closest to him. To gain pleasure and self-confidence, he challenged himself in sports and other interests. In particular, he found comfort and enjoyment in the one area that would stay with him throughout his life—the theater. His greatest need was to feel he was part of a family. In acting, he found a satisfying substitute for that feeling.

Christopher Reeve was born on September 25, 1952, at Lenox Hill Hospital in New York City. His parents were well educated and came from prominent families. His mother, Barbara Pitney Lamb, was the daughter of a successful New York lawyer. His father, Franklin D'Olier Reeve, a poet and college professor in Slavic languages, traced his family's roots back to the year 1214, first in France and then Ireland. When the D'Oliers came to the United States in the 1800s, they settled in Philadelphia and became rich by founding and owning several cotton mills. Christopher's great-grandfather, Franklin D'Olier, was one of the founders of the American Legion, a veterans organization.

Amassing greater wealth, however, was not important to Franklin Reeve. Neither were the ties that bound him to his family. As Christopher later said of his father, "He reacted against all that [family] privilege by cutting himself off from it."[1]

Franklin Reeve had just graduated from Princeton University in Princeton, New Jersey, in 1950 when he met Barbara Lamb,

11

who was then a student at Vassar, the prestigious all-girls school in Poughkeepsie, New York. They married the following year, when he was twenty-three and she was eighteen, and moved to New York City, where Franklin began studying for a master's degree in Russian language at Columbia University. The young couple lived in a small apartment near the campus. Franklin, refusing to accept help from his wealthy family, earned money for tuition by working as a waiter and laborer.

Two years later, Mrs. Reeve gave birth to a blue-eyed, blond-haired boy. They named him Christopher but called him "Toph" or "Tophy" for short. The following year a second son, Benjamin, was born, and nicknamed "Beejy." The boys developed a brotherly friendship as they grew older, though they were always very competitive with each other. Christopher and his brother often displayed the sort of rivalry common among siblings who are close in age. "Ben and I were usually going at each other, competing for attention and space,"[2] Reeve later wrote. They were also often mischievous and a handful for their young mother.

The End of Christopher's First Family

Christopher's parents appeared to be an ideal, happy couple. However, their marriage began to fail after only a short time, possibly because they were two very different people with few similar interests.

Christopher's mother was mainly interested in being a good housewife and raising a family. His father, however, had a passion for politics and social causes she did not share. He saw every action—even his work—as a chance to make a political statement. Reeve later explained to one interviewer:

> My father was both a [student of] Slavic languages [by day, at Columbia University] and a laborer unloading banana boats in Hoboken at night. He did it to make ends meet and also as a political involvement. He was very intrigued by the labor movement. He felt himself a worker in the masses.[3]

The young Reeve turned to the theater and athletics to escape family strife.

Franklin Reeve's interest in the woman he married was gradually replaced by his interest in his work and colleagues, both on the wharves and at the university; the couple gradually drifted apart. In his autobiography Reeve recalled that his parents had little in common. "My mother was never an intellectual, and before long they had little to talk about. The atmosphere in our home became increasingly tense."[4]

Eventually the strains on the marriage became too great. When Christopher was not yet four years old, his mother left his father. On New Year's Eve, 1955, she took Christopher and his brother to Princeton, New Jersey, where her parents lived. They paid the rent for a house there for her and the two boys. Eventually, she was able to support herself and her sons by working as a writer and assistant editor for a local weekly newspaper, *Town Topics*.

Christopher's father remained at Columbia, where he completed work for his master's and doctorate degrees in Russian language. Eventually, he took a faculty position at Wesleyan University in Middletown, Connecticut.

The Reeves' divorce was a bitter one, and neither spoke to the other for fifteen years. Their breakup was especially hard on their sons, who lived with their mother but were allowed to visit their father on alternate weekends and holidays and for six weeks in the summer.

Christopher felt caught in the middle of his parents' bitter feelings for each other. As he later explained to an interviewer:

> My father and mother were always fighting over me, and therefore canceled each other out. Consequently, I grew up not wanting to depend on them or anybody else. That's probably the key to my personality.[5]

Not feeling part of a family anymore after his parents divorced, Christopher responded by alternately retreating inside himself or by keeping himself busy. At the age of five, for example, he pleaded with his mother to let him play ice hockey on the city of Princeton's Pee Wee hockey team. Although she thought it a dangerous sport for a little boy, she let him have his way. Christopher would get up early every Saturday morning and be at the ice rink, dressed and practicing skating and shooting hockey pucks across the ice.

Christopher was determined to get in the games, and even at that young age, he showed his tenacity. Again and again he begged the coach to let him play. All the other positions were already taken, so the coach let him be a goalie.

In sports and other activities, Christopher found refuge from the pain his parents' divorce caused him. Soon, he added to his arsenal of ways to forget his broken family. He learned to play the piano and swim, to ski at the age of six, and sail at the age of seven.

Although he was active in sports, Christopher was sometimes a sickly child. Oftentimes, he suffered from asthma and allergies that made breathing difficult. At an early age, for example, he discovered he was allergic to horses and could not go near one without wheezing. In addition to his allergies, he developed alopecia areata, a disorder of the nervous system that sometimes caused

The Young Adventurer

From an early age, Christopher Reeve sought adventure and challenge, especially in sports and other activities. "I loved taking risks," he says in *Still Me*. "Whether on-stage or as a goalie on the hockey team, I kept putting myself on the line."

After learning to ski at age six and sail a boat at age seven, when he was eleven he imitated daredevil motorcycle racing while riding his bicycle. He pretended he was Steve McQueen, who became his boyhood hero after he saw the actor's exciting motorcycle riding in the 1963 movie about World War II, *The Great Escape*. It nearly cost Reeve his life when one day while racing his bicycle on a highway without wearing a helmet, he was almost killed by a truck.

some of his hair to fall out and leave patchy bald spots. This condition would plague him into adulthood. These health problems were troublesome, but at least Christopher's family difficulties seemed to be easing as time went on.

A Second Family

In June 1959, when Christopher was nearly seven years old and busy in school and sports, his mother married a wealthy Princeton investment banker, Tristam B. Johnson. Christopher then found himself to be a member of a new family. He wondered if this family would be happier and more lasting than the first.

His mother's remarriage came with some complications, however. His new father had been married before and already had four children by his first wife. Christopher now not only had a new father but two stepbrothers, Tristam Jr., and Tom, and two stepsisters, Beth and Kate. However, he rarely saw them because they lived in Utah with their mother. And within a few years, his mother and new father had two children of their own, which meant that Christopher would be growing up with two half brothers, Jeffrey and Kevin. With a wide difference in age between themselves and their half brothers, Christopher and Ben spent little time with Jeffrey and Kevin.

By this time, Christopher's father had also remarried. Franklin Reeve and his second wife, Helen, then had three children together—first a daughter, Alison, then two sons, Mark and Brock.

The remarriages of both his parents required a lot of adjustment for Christopher. For one thing, his life had gotten crowded. He had gone from having one family and one brother to two families and a brother plus six half or stepbrothers and three half or stepsisters.

Christopher regarded his stepfather as kind but strict. He did not permit the children to watch television or read comic books.

Even before they were teenagers, however, neither Christopher nor his brother Ben felt completely happy in their new family, and they reacted to this by getting into mischief. Ben would often stay out late or not even come home some nights. Several times, Christopher took his parents' car for spins without them knowing about it, and once he "borrowed" a neighbor's motorboat for a ride on the nearby bay. Another time, he went to a boat cabin with a cigarette, a beer, and a girlfriend several years older than he. "Obviously," he wrote later, "my mother was right: I was in a hurry to grow up."[6]

A rebellious young man, Reeve occasionally got into mischief.

After a few years, Christopher began to worry that things might not be going well with his mother's second marriage. His stepfather began staying away from home, and once again it seemed that his family was in trouble. As an adult, Reeve recalled:

> The table would be set, and he wouldn't show up. He would disappear for a couple of days at a time without any explanation, without even saying that he owed us an explanation. I had hopes that this little family would take hold, particularly when my half brothers, Jeff and Kevin, came along. But it didn't work; it wouldn't jell. We weren't able to come together under one roof.[7]

Things did not improve when the family moved into a larger house. "Jeff and Kevin kept to themselves up on the third floor," Reeve wrote. "Ben and I were separated by a long hallway as well as our natural jealousy of each other. My mother and Tris were experiencing the beginning of the end."[8]

School Days

Despite their strained relationship, Christopher's mother and stepfather stayed together for twenty-five years of marriage. Tristam Johnson tried to be a good parent by seeing that his stepsons got a good education. Johnson enrolled both Christopher and Benjamin in Princeton Country Day School, a private, all-boys school where they spent their elementary and middle-school years. Founded as a school for the sons of professors at Princeton University, it maintained a very formal atmosphere; students always wore a dark blue sport coat and tie to classes.

Christopher loved school, and his instructors found him to be a cooperative student who tried hard to excel in everything he did. He was often first in his class academically and very good in sports as well.

An activity Christopher especially liked was an after-school father-son carpentry workshop where he and his stepfather built things together such as little birdhouses. His stepfather also supported Christopher in his sporting activities. He recalled later,

Playing the "All-American Boy"

Christopher Reeve may not have been aware of it, but even at a young age, some of his real life was really acting. At school he acted the part of being the "All-American Boy." That is typically someone who is good looking, clean-cut, good in both studies and sports, friendly and cheerful and, definitely, well adjusted. In reality, teenage Christopher met only a few of the qualifications. As he told Sharon Begley for the July 1, 1996, issue of *Newsweek:* "When I was a kid, I never cracked a smile. Acting was a way to help me loosen up, and relax."

Christopher hid his inner insecurity by playing the role of a well-adjusted student in both grammar and high school. He even fooled his teachers. In *Christopher Reeve,* a book by Libby Hughes, Princeton Country Day School teacher Wesley McCaughan says, "I remember him as a delightful young boy, a good student, cooperative, and respected by the boys. In high school, if you passed him in the corridors, he always greeted you with a big grin. He was an all-American boy."

Acting enabled Christopher to step outside himself and forget that he sometimes might be unhappy or anxious in real life. In an interview with Margery Steinberg for the October 1995 issue of *People* magazine he explained: "Being someone else took me away from a lot of things I was not prepared to deal with."

Onstage, in school, and when engaged in sports, Christopher Reeve appeared to be the all-American boy. But he was really only acting the part.

Few would suspect that the clean-cut, good-looking Reeve lacked self-assurance.

"Tris came to watch my soccer and hockey games. I developed a great affection for him. Yet this was complicated by the fact that what I wanted most was my [natural] father's approval."[9]

By excelling, Christopher hoped to please Franklin Reeve. Despite his fondness for his stepfather, Christopher desperately wanted his own father's love and approval, which was always tied to performance. If he did well in something, his father would show some affection. His stepfather, on the other hand, did not put any conditions on their relationship.

But Franklin Reeve's growing involvement in political causes and his remarriage left little time for visits from Christopher and Benjamin. This saddened Christopher because he had always looked forward to visiting his father, especially when they went sailing together off Long Island Sound. Christopher was good at sailing and enjoyed it. While still just a boy, he began entering sailboat races.

Christopher also enjoyed summer vacations with his mother and stepfather's family because they stayed at the large house owned by his stepfather's brother in the New Jersey shore town of Bay Head. The house could sleep twenty-seven people and stood among sand dunes facing the Atlantic Ocean. Christopher joined the family at the local yacht club, sailing in races on nearby lakes and on the ocean. Sailing became a very important part of young Christopher's life.

Yet, time spent with his two families brought up many conflicting feelings for Christopher. While he was with his father and tried to behave and perform well so as to win his approval and affection, he often thought about his stepfather's unconditional love. While he was with his stepfather, he compared him with his father.

And then there was his mother. Even though Christopher saw less of his father, he felt closer to him than he did to his mother. While he loved her, he felt she allowed others to dominate her. He considered this tendency a character weakness and was determined that he would not allow that to happen to him.

The Play's the Thing

In the spring of 1962, when Christopher was nine, a major turning point occurred in his life. A talent scout from the prestigious

Young Christopher Was Not "Super" with Girls

During his teen years, Christopher was shy and awkward, both physically and with girls. He seldom asked them for a date, because he did not want to risk being rejected.

Christopher found acting to be the answer to what to do about girls. In an interview with Sarah Matthiessen for the October 1980 issue of *After Dark* magazine, he recalled that as a teenager, acting solved the problem of what to do on Friday and Saturday nights.

"I didn't have to worry about how I was going to ask little Suzy out for a date," Reeve said, "because I was too busy with the theater anyway. I was very tall and physically awkward. I was six foot two inches tall by the time I was fourteen. And I moved like a building. Even though I was attractive, I lacked self-confidence. The theater was a nice place to go to solve those problems."

Reeve solved his "date night" dilemma by performing in plays. Here, a photo from his Princeton Country Day School yearbook shows Reeve in Little Mary Sunshine.

McCarter Theater in Princeton came to his school looking for a boy to sing a small role in the stage company's production of the Gilbert and Sullivan operetta *The Yeomen of the Guard.* Christopher could sing, a little, and was eager to try a new adventure. From his seat in a fourth grade class, he raised his hand anxiously. He was tested and given a small part. This was his first onstage experience, and he discovered right away that he loved the theater. "It was absolute magic to me, and I wanted to be part of it," [10] he recalled years later in an interview.

After that introduction, Christopher tried out for every part he could get in school plays. His passion for acting even exceeded his love of sports. "It was one thing to be a good student-athlete, but acting was even better," [11] he later wrote. School dramas presented an extra challenge to members of the cast. Since Princeton Country Day School was an all-boy school during Christopher's early years there, all the parts in a play had to be played by boys, not girls, so he sometimes played women, often characters a lot older than he. The challenge of playing such roles gave him a chance to become a more versatile actor; moreover, it took his mind even farther away from his unhappy home life.

Young Christopher found himself completely hooked on acting. At the age of twelve, he played a sixty-five-year-old woman housekeeper in Agatha Christie's *Witness for the Prosecution*, and one scene in particular got loud applause from the audience. "Right in the middle of the first act," Christopher remembered. "It went straight to my head, and I thought, this is wonderful." [12]

With his enthusiasm for theater, Christopher became president of his high school drama club. He also won major roles in many school plays, including the dramas *Our Town, Picnic,* and *Watch on the Rhine.* Besides possessing a talent for acting, Christopher had developed into an accomplished singer. In the musical comedies *The Boy Friend* and *Little Mary Sunshine,* the boy soprano was told he had a wonderful voice.

A New Family

In addition to acting in school plays, Christopher was soon cast in small parts with the professional repertory stage company at the McCarter Theater. For the first time in his life, Christopher

Reeve (second from the left) in Watch on the Rhine *(photo from the Princeton Country Day School yearbook).*

felt that he was part of a group whose members respected and accepted each other and worked together toward a common goal. As he later wrote:

> It [the McCarter Theater] felt like a family. I was part of a group of people who worked together every day on projects they believed in. All the horses were pulling the wagon in the same direction, toward opening night. I loved the whole atmosphere. No strife, no tension here, at least none that I could see. I behaved myself and tried hard, and the adults liked me. Right there was the beginning of a way to escape the conflicting feelings I had about my two families. I'm sure that's why I became an actor.[13]

Reeve said he felt the McCarter Theater was his home base, where he felt most secure. Something else about acting appealed to Christopher. While he was competitive and wanted to excel in anything he did, he also wanted to be very good at something on his own; something that had no ties to his four parents, his brother, or his stepbrothers, stepsisters, half brothers, and half sister. Acting was a profession that nobody in his family had tried before, and that appealed to his independent nature.

Chapter 2

From Apprentice Actor to Superman

Reeve's natural acting ability, a determination to master the craft of acting, plus his good looks, propelled him in less than a decade to a promising stage career and his first part in a movie. Then came an audition for the role that every actor in Hollywood wanted and that would change his life.

Bitten by the Acting Bug

There was no question in teenage Christopher's mind . . . he loved acting and wanted to learn to be a really good actor. That meant spending as much time as he could around the stage, and an opportunity to do just that presented itself.

In the summer of 1968, when he was fifteen, Reeve became an apprentice at the prestigious Williamstown Theater Festival on the Williams College campus in the small New England town of Williamstown, Massachusetts. There he took drama classes, helped build stage sets, moved props, and sold tickets in the theater's box office. Thus began a very happy lifelong relationship with the Williamstown Theater.

"That summer [at the Williamstown Theater Festival] marked the beginning of my independence," Reeve later wrote. "Apprentices were needed from the middle of June right through Labor Day, so there would be no time to visit either of my families, which I have to admit was a relief."[14]

Christopher joined about sixty young men and women as apprentices at Williamstown. "We did everything," he recalled. "Hung lights, painted scenery, attended classes in acting, voice and movement."[15]

Reeve needed to take lessons in movement, as he later told an interviewer. "I was very tall and physically awkward. I had a disease called Osgood Schlatter's disease, which prevents your tendons from keeping up with the rate of growth of your bones. You have a lot of fluid in your joints, and you don't move terribly well. As a result, I was very, very awkward. And enormous. I used to stand with my legs locked all the time. I was six-two by the time I was fourteen." [16]

Christopher learned to act and move onstage well enough to get parts at the summer theater. Because there were eight plays to produce in a ten-week season and only fifteen Equity—that is, professional, unionized—actors in the company, apprentices were sometimes cast in parts, and Christopher was among them.

Peter Hunt, then a lighting designer and later a theater and television director, said years later, "I remember Chris as extremely nice and good-looking. Sigourney Weaver, now a famous actress, was an apprentice, too. I had a good feeling about

Reeve Finds a New "Family"

Christopher Reeve found in the acting company of the Williamstown Theater many of the things he lacked in his real-life family, as he explained years later in an interview for the Bravo Cable Channel television series *Inside the Actors Studio:*

"That repertory family—real repertory—they became a family. And I was between families in my own life. To be adopted by that family, and to think of theater as a place where people of diverse talent and interests came together to make—hopefully—art, which often was the case, was a real privilege. They adopted me—took me in—and it was a place of great security and great growth. I look back with great fondness there."

The one stable place in Reeve's life became the theater. "It was all just bits and pieces," he said in an interview with Roger Rosenblatt for the August 26, 1996, issue of *Time* magazine. "You don't want to risk getting involved with people for fear that things are going to fall apart. That's why I found relief in playing characters. You knew where you were, in fiction. You knew where you stood."

Reeve would return to the Williamstown Theater many times in his career, performing in plays there for very little money even after he became a famous movie star.

both of them. When you see kids coming through, you can tell which ones will succeed and their careers take off."[17]

When Reeve turned sixteen, he became a member of the Actors' Equity Association, the actors' union, and hired an agent. His agent soon got him his first paid job as an actor, in Turgenev's *A Month in the Country* at the Harvard Summer School Repertory Theater in Cambridge, Massachusetts. His salary was forty-four dollars a week, half of which went for dorm rent. In the following summers he performed at the Boothbay Playhouse in Maine and the San Diego Shakespeare Festival in California.

The Actor in College

As his graduation from Princeton Country Day School neared, Reeve increased his extracurricular activities. Besides acting in more plays and playing hockey, he sang in a madrigal group

Reeve (back row, left) was well liked by his classmates. Here he performed with the madrigal singing group (photo from the Princeton Country Day School yearbook).

and worked on the school's literary magazine. He also continued taking piano lessons and became assistant conductor of the
school orchestra.

Now Reeve had a big decision to make regarding his future.
He thought he might skip college and begin a full-time acting career. But his mother and stepfather insisted he get a college education first, and to please them he did what they asked.

Where to attend college was also a question to be settled.
Partly because his stepfather was a Yale graduate, Reeve applied
there, and also to Cornell University because he liked both its
theater arts department and its academic program. Yale turned

him down, but he was ac-
cepted to Cornell. He liked its
academic program and knew
it would also please his grandfather, Richard Reeve, who
had gone there.

Because he wanted a well-
rounded education, Reeve decided his major would not be
theater, but rather English and
music theory. He refused to
avoid the tough courses. "I believe in the old-fashioned kind
of education," he told a writer
years later. "Studying science
and math gives you the discipline to take on challenges."[18]

Located in Ithaca, New
York, Cornell was a good
choice of college for an aspir-

*Cornell University provided an
opportunity for Reeve to explore his
interests and develop mental
discipline.*

ing actor. It was close enough to New York City to allow Reeve
to drive there in his 1970 Fiat and audition for plays there when
he had time.

"I had an understanding agent who'd set up auditions
around my class schedule," he later told an interviewer. He
would cut classes for a day and make appointments for movie
and television auditions, then would go back to Cornell and

make up the homework. "Somehow I managed to balance the academic and professional sides of my life."[19]

Christopher's main after-school activity would be acting, but he also found time for dating. He had dated girls in high school and had had a crush or two, but his first steady girlfriend was a pretty Cornell English and music theory major, Jennifer Shea.

"Chris had a drive and a dream," Shea recalled years later. "He had the drive to achieve his goals for a career in the professional theater. It was clear what he wanted, and he was not afraid of hard work."[20]

Reeve also impressed his teachers. Steve Cole, one of his drama professors at Cornell, said about him as a student, "Chris was the most decent, interesting, and sweet guy. He was generous and not conceited. He was well-loved by his fellow students and colleagues."[21]

Reeve was beginning to learn his craft. He received his best review as the romantic leading man in a poetic play, *Life Is a Dream*. He learned even more about acting during summer vacations when he toured in comedies with two established stars, Eleanor Parker in *40 Carats* and Celeste Holm in *The Irregular Verb to Love*.

Meanwhile, there was plenty of activity going on at Cornell and other college campuses all over America for students to take an interest in. It was a time of social and political unrest, when

The Actor's Life for Christopher

Even while in college, many young people do not know what career to follow or what life's work to pursue. Christopher Reeve did not have this dilemma.

Adrian Havill, in his biography of Reeve, *Man of Steel,* quotes him as saying, "I knew very early on that I wanted to be an actor. I was saved a lot of soul-searching—who am I, what am I going to do with my life? Acting is what I do best.

"The luckiest thing that happened to me was that my parents let me take responsibility for my own life from the time I was thirteen."

"He had drive," Havill quotes Reeve's mother saying. "He was self-directed; he seemed happy only when he was in a play. Nearly everything he's done has been to improve his acting."

students on many college campuses protested against the Vietnam War and flocked to rock concerts chanting "Give peace a chance."

Reeve's activist father would have joined the protesters, but the young actor did not. His main focus was learning to become a better actor and establishing a residence hall at Cornell for acting majors.

While at Cornell, Reeve sadly learned where he stood with his father, as he recalled later:

> Once during my freshman year at Cornell, I drove over to his house in Connecticut for the weekend. He was very distant, and I had to spend most of the time talking with my stepmother. Then, at one point, I abruptly asked him "Do you care? Do you care what happens to me?" And he said, "Frankly, Toph, less and less." It was a pretty honest thing to say, it was certainly what I was experiencing, but that's something you never forget. But I adored my father, and he did have a strong influence on me.[22]

Time Out for Europe

Once Reeve had completed his sophomore year, Cornell allowed him to spend part of his junior year abroad. Reeve was always eager to learn about other cultures, and he especially wanted to go to Europe, to soak up its culture and theater.

As part of his academic experience, Reeve became a backstage observer at the prestigious Old Vic Theatre in London, where he saw Sir Laurence Olivier and other great British actors perform. "I was hired as a 'dogsbody,'" he later recalled. "That's a glorified errand boy. I also worked [behind the scenes] on the first British production of *Equus,* and had a grand time."[23]

From London, Reeve went to Paris and hung around the famous Comédie-Française, watching rehearsals of a classic Molière play. He later said that because he spoke French, he talked to some of the French actors and backstage workers.

Before he knew it, Reeve almost became a Frenchman, as he later recalled: "I took to wearing a fisherman's sweater and baggy pants, and spent many afternoons in a bar smoking a pipe

Reeve's experience as a backstage errand-runner at the Old Vic Theatre in London strengthened his determination to become a serious actor.

and writing in my journal. I have no idea who I thought I was, but I was still experimenting with different identities, both on-stage and off."[24]

Even before returning to Cornell, to write a thesis about his experiences at the famous repertory companies, Reeve had come to an important decision regarding his own future. "The trip to Europe had strengthened my desire to become a serious classical actor," he later wrote, "and I felt I couldn't wait any longer."[25]

But he needed more training if he was to become a classical actor and act in the Greek plays of Aeschylus, Sophocles, Euripides, and Aristophanes, and those of Shakespeare and others. And he knew where to get it.

Juilliard Drama School

In 1973, Cornell granted academic credit to Reeve for spending his senior year attending the advanced acting program of the Drama Division of the prestigious Juilliard School in New York City. This began what Reeve later said he considered to be the most exciting period of his acting life until then. Juilliard enabled him to perfect his talent by learning more about the art of acting from some of the best drama coaches and directors in the country. The program's graduates often go on to become major stars in film. Among his classmates were fledgling actors Robin Williams, William Hurt, and Mandy Patinkin.

A Lifelong Friendship

Reeve began a lifelong friendship with a fellow actor who became his roommate at the Juilliard School, as he later wrote in *Still Me*:

> The first person I met at Juilliard was the other advanced student, a short, stocky, long-haired fellow from Marin County, California, who wore tie-dyed shirts with track suit bottoms and talked a mile a minute.
>
> I'd never seen so much energy contained in one person. He was like an untied balloon that had been inflated and immediately released.
>
> I watched in awe as he virtually caromed off the walls of the classrooms and hallways. To say that he was "on" would be a major understatement. There was never a moment when he wasn't doing voices, imitating teachers, and making our faces ache from laughing at his antics. His name, of course, was Robin Williams.
>
> Robin Williams would go on to star in many big-budget Hollywood films and won the 1998 Academy Award for best supporting actor in *Good Will Hunting*.

Robin Williams and Christopher Reeve.

Reeve's year at Juilliard did much to build his range as an actor. Under some of the nation's leading drama coaches, he learned to read lines and use his voice properly as an actor. He studied pantomime to improve his ability to act without speaking. For improved agility he learned fencing, stage fighting, acrobatics, and even some ballet.

Besides offering him a wide range of experience, Juilliard exposed Reeve to some of the most talented actors of the day. For example, one of the acting teachers at Juilliard who took special interest in Reeve was John Houseman, who had combined teaching with a career in the theater, movies, and television. Houseman was recognized by his peers as a superb actor; his performance in the movie *The Paper Chase* as an outwardly gruff law professor with an inwardly soft heart won him the 1973 Academy Award as best supporting actor.

Among the faculty members at Juilliard was actor John Houseman, shown here in a scene from The Paper Chase.

Cornell awarded Reeve a Bachelor of Arts degree in English and music upon completion of his year at Julliard in 1974. Eager to stay on at Juilliard and earn a master's degree in acting, he needed money for tuition, so he tried out for any professional acting role he could get.

After playing the lead role of Macheath ("Mack the Knife") in *The Three-Penny Opera* at Harvard Summer Repertory Theater, Reeve moved back to New York City and rented a fourth-floor walk-up apartment he described as "a hole in the wall."[26] He furnished it with furniture others had thrown out with the trash, and his bed was just a mattress on the floor.

It was during his Juilliard year that Reeve fell in love—with flying. Somehow, he found enough money to pay for flying lessons, got his private pilot's license, and bought a used Cherokee 140 for eight thousand dollars.

Whenever he had the time, Reeve would fly his plane around the country just for the adventure of it and the learning experiences he gained from the trips. "I used to go everywhere in that little airplane and camp out," he told an interviewer. "I went to Burlington, Vermont; London, Ontario—all those little towns on the way to Chicago—then down to New Orleans. I parked in grass fields every night and camped out with a sleeping bag.

"I get a big kick out of dropping into Amarillo [Texas], or wherever, and meeting some waitress who has an accent and a pencil in her hair. I wouldn't run into these people normally. I just love coming down after three or four hours in the sky and being someplace else."[27]

Soap Opera Success

Eager to get more acting experience, when no stage role was forthcoming for him, Reeve auditioned for a small part in a television soap opera, *Love of Life*. He won the role of Ben Harper, a charming bigamist.

For two years, Reeve played the part of the womanizer almost too well. One day while he was lunching in a Manhattan restaurant an angry woman fan of the series came up to his table and hit him over the head with her purse. Also, his look-alike

Reeve made a habit of flying around the country in search of new experiences.

brother, Benjamin, was mistaken for him one day by a woman who pounded him on the back with her umbrella.

While continuing to act in *Love of Life,* Reeve also appeared onstage in New York, at the Circle Repertory Theater and the Manhattan Club. It was about this time that he was presented the opportunity to work with one of the all-time greats of stage and film. In 1975, he landed a small role in the Broadway play *A Matter of Gravity,* playing the grandson of the star, Katharine Hepburn, one of the theater's and movies' greatest actresses. The play ran only two months on Broadway, but it gave Reeve more confidence and his best acting notice yet.

The experience also led to a close friendship with Hepburn, although Reeve was intimidated by her personality and reputation as an actress. When he was later asked in a television interview how it felt to act with Katharine Hepburn, he replied with a grin, "You don't act *with* Katharine Hepburn. You act *near* Katharine Hepburn."[28]

Hepburn took an interest in Reeve and tried to advise the young actor. "She invested so much time in me, always pushing me to do more," Reeve recalls. "She was 67 and I was 22. I adored her, but she scared the pants off me most of the time."[29]

Reeve found Hepburn's instruction useful, if difficult, to carry out. "She often used to say to me, 'Be fascinating, Christopher, be fascinating.' I used to think, 'That's easy for you to do; the rest of us have to work at it.'"[30]

Hollywood Calls

When *A Matter of Gravity* closed, Reeve was again at loose ends, as most actors are between acting jobs. The movies then beckoned Reeve, but not on a large scale. He went to Hollywood in 1976 to act in a small role in the submarine drama *Gray Lady Down*, starring Charlton Heston. The film was not successful, however, and Reeve's small part in the film was hardly noticed.

When no other movie offers came his way, Reeve returned to New York and looked for more work on the stage. It was in late January 1977, while he was appearing in a small part as a grandfather in an off-Broadway play called *My Life*, that a phone call from his agent would change his life.

Reeve learned that movie producers Alexander Salkind and his son Ilya Salkind were auditioning actors to play the title role in their new big-budget movie, *Superman*. Their first choice had been Robert Redford, but he had turned them down. So had their second choice, Paul Newman, and they themselves had turned down Warren Beatty, Burt Reynolds, and dozens of other major Hollywood leading men. In the end, they decided to search for a tall, dark, handsome—but unknown—young actor to play the hero.

The Salkinds remembered photos of a young actor that casting director Lynn Stalmaster kept sending them. Stalmaster had been casting director on *Gray Lady Down*, and had been impressed by Reeve's stage credentials in addition to his leading-man good looks. As casting director for *Superman*, he thought Reeve might be just right for the part. Sending Reeve's photo to the movie's producers paid off, and the Salkinds thought they might as well audition the young actor.

Brushes with Death

Reeve's love of flying both planes and gliders sometimes nearly cost him his life in air accidents, whether he was responsible for them or not.

While taking time off from filming *Superman* in England in 1978 he crash-landed a plane in a field near the village of Watlington because of bad weather. Two years later, during a break from the filming of *Superman II,* he crash-landed a glider on a British airfield.

During the filming of a 1983 ABC-TV special on stuntmen, *Celebrity Daredevils,* a small plane accidentally roared straight at Reeve. It passed over his head, inches from his face.

The following year, Reeve cheated death on Martha's Vineyard in Massachusetts while parasailing. His chute had broken loose, and he fell more than a hundred feet into shallow water. Fortunately, he walked away with only bruised ribs.

Reeve took each accident in stride, as Adrian Havill quoted him in his book *Man of Steel*: "A little danger adds up to a lot of excitement. What good is it to go through life without ever taking risks?"

When Reeve first learned the part was that of Superman in a movie version of the comic book and former television series, he was not very interested. He preferred to wait for more dignified stage or movie roles.

Although undecided about wanting to play Superman, Reeve agreed to an audition for the part, mainly on the principle that an actor should never turn down an audition. He met with Ilya Salkind and the movie's director, Richard Donner, at the Sherry Netherland Hotel in New York City. At first look, they were not impressed. Reeve not only looked too inexperienced as an actor, he also looked too young, too tall, and not muscular enough to play Superman.

Donner then had an idea. After all, the actor who played Superman also had to play Clark Kent, the newspaper reporter. Donner handed Reeve a pair of horn-rimmed glasses and asked him to impersonate Superman's alter ego. Reeve put on the glasses, which made him look intellectual, and also rounded his shoulders in a slouch so he looked meek, the opposite of confident Superman. Salkind and Donner were so impressed that they offered to pay Reeve's airfare to London for a screen test.

On the plane to London, Reeve read the script for *Superman* and liked it a lot. He could see possibilities for playing both the caped crusader and the newspaper reporter with some character nuances and subtle humor.

But he remained conflicted. Did he want to play Superman? Stage friends warned that playing a comic book hero in the movies could ruin his career because audiences and drama critics might not take his stage work seriously afterward.

He also wondered what his natural father would think of his playing a comic book hero. He worried, too, about what the rest of his family would say. But which family? By then, Reeve felt he had at least three families: his mother, brother, and real father; his stepfather and half sister and brothers; and his adopted acting "family." If he got the part and played Superman, which family would he please the most, or let down the most? More important, would he let himself down?

Chapter 3

Fame and Personal Fortune

P LAYING SUPERMAN BROUGHT Christopher Reeve overnight fame and big paychecks, but his personal fortunes were not as successful. Distrustful of relationships because of his parents' divorce, he fell in love but was reluctant to marry. His movie career after *Superman* disappointed him; then after several years it took an upward turn. So did his personal life, as his first relationship ended and a second one began.

Something to Like in Superman

Flying to London to take a screen test to play Superman, Christopher Reeve had more doubts about playing the role. "At first I was kind of a snob and thought it was beneath me," he recalled in a television interview. "After all, I was a classical actor."[31]

Fellow actors cautioned that the role might typecast him as an action hero, which could spoil his career as a serious actor. But Reeve saw this as a challenge that appealed to him, as he later told a reporter: "Maybe that's what intrigued me about it. The risks [to his career that playing Superman] involved."[32]

To prepare for his screen test, Reeve thought about how he would play Superman. The part was written in an understated way, and he believed he could play the superhero with some gentleness and vulnerability.

A very important idea then came to Reeve as he reread the script. He explained in *Still Me:* "When Lois Lane asks, 'Who are you?,' Superman simply responds, 'A friend.' I felt that was the key to the part: I tried to downplay being a hero and emphasize being a friend."[33]

He also decided to pattern Superman's alter ego, Clark Kent, the unseasoned newspaper reporter, after Cary Grant in the 1938 comedy classic *Bringing Up Baby,* one of his favorite early Katharine Hepburn movies. He would play Kent as bashful and clumsy, as a contrast with Superman's confidence and heroic bearing.

For his screen test as Clark Kent, Reeve wore a gray flannel suit, his sandy hair was blackened and slicked down, and he wore dark-rimmed glasses. He played the inexperienced newspaperman as shy and awkward, but with just the right touch of sincerity. When he tested as Superman, he donned the cape and put on the boots he was given, but was still too thin to fill the body suit of the superhero, so it was heavily padded.

Reeve's part in Superman *presented a new kind of risk: that he might be typecast forever as the famous superhero.*

Reeve did not know what the Salkinds or Donner thought of his screen test but he got a clue from someone else, as he wrote later. "Sheer adrenaline carried me through the screen test. On the way back to my hotel my driver [the Salkinds' movie studio's chauffeur] said, 'I'm not supposed to tell you this, but you've got the part.'"[34]

Back in New York a week later, Reeve was startled to hear movie gossip columnist Rona Barrett announce on television that he had been selected to play Superman. He phoned the Salkinds in London for confirmation, and Ilya Salkind said it was true.

Reeve then signed a fifty-two-week contract for $250,000, a fortune to the young actor despite that Marlon Brando got a million dollars for his small role as Superman's father. Reeve's salary would escalate if *Superman* was a success and he starred in future sequels.

In typical fashion, Reeve downplayed the role talent played in landing the part. He told reporters during filming that the role came to him not because of acting talent, but because he looked like Superman in the comic books.

When Reeve phoned his mother about the good news, she was overjoyed. His father's reaction was something else. When Reeve told him he was going to play the part of Superman, his intellectual father at first thought he was referring to the role in the classic play *Man and Superman* by George Bernard Shaw, and was very pleased. But when Reeve explained it was the comic book character, his father responded with an embarrassed silence. Reeve's mother and stepfather flew to London and watched some of the filming of the movie, but Franklin Reeve stayed away.

In addition to using his intellect in playing his challenging roles, Reeve had to apply physical effort. He gained forty pounds and exercised to build up the appropriate Superman muscles.

On the set of *Superman* he was all business, although he played both the caped crusader and Clark Kent with some humor. He knew he had to be very good in both roles, or the movie would fail. "I approached the role seriously," Reeve later wrote. "I always flatly refused any invitation to mock the Superman character or send him up."[35]

Reeve had to build himself up physically to fill his role as the muscular Superman. For his audition, he wore a padded suit to make him look muscular.

Making the movie was a demanding job, although he enjoyed it. "Filming *Superman* was sometimes tedious and exasperating," Reeve said. "I spent months hanging on wires for brief moments in the movie that would then have to be reshot. But ultimately it was a wonderful experience."[36]

"I did my own stunts," Reeve recalled in a television interview. "I was really foolish. When I put on that [Superman] costume, I was dangerous, to myself. I used to think, if the wires would break, I'd keep flying."[37]

Those physical risks were real: both he and Margot Kidder, who played his love interest, Lois Lane, hung in a harness 240 feet above New York's East River as part of the filming of their flying scenes.

Years later, in an interview, Reeve looked back on his experience with humor and downplayed the amount of work shooting *Superman* had involved. "Perhaps the hardest part about playing Superman was the costume," Reeve said. "It had no pockets. What can you do with your hands?"[38]

Performing his own stunts in Superman, *Reeve now says, was "really foolish."*

As Superman, Reeve was supposed to be invulnerable. In real life, however, he proved to be as vulnerable to the slings and arrows of life as anyone else.

Love Trips Up Superman

While in his Superman costume during a break in filming at Pinewood studio outside London in October 1977, Reeve went to the commissary for a snack. Standing in the serving line, he accidentally stepped backward and his heel crunched the toe of a tall, attractive young woman with long ash blond hair, who was standing behind him. Gae Exton was British and in the studio that day as part of her work in management for a London modeling and casting agency.

Unlike the plot of a romantic movie, however, Reeve did not sweep Exton off her feet after stepping on one of them. "The first thing I noticed were his blue eyes—he has those incredibly piercing blue eyes," Gae Exton told an interviewer several years later. "But it wasn't love at first sight." [39]

A few weeks later, they met again at a luncheon and Reeve asked her for a date. His attraction to Exton, who was separated from her businessman husband, grew. After a few months of dating, she moved into Reeve's rented London apartment.

The couple kept their romance a secret for more than a year, until Reeve took her with him to the British Royal Family's benefit premier of *Superman*. He denied rumors that he was reluctant to marry Exton because of his parents' divorce when he was a boy.

The couple did not marry, but their son, Matthew, was born in 1979 and daughter, Alexandra, in 1983.

International Success

Superman—the Movie met with overwhelming success upon its release in theaters in December 1978. Critics, moviegoers, and diehard Superman fans all praised the movie and Reeve's dual performances as "the Man of Steel" and his human counterpart.

Reeve in his role as father—with his son, Matthew, and girlfriend Gae Exton.

Critics Praise Reeve as Superman

Superman—the Movie became one of the box-office hits of 1978. Even a critic as difficult to please as Pauline Kael of the *New Yorker* magazine, who did not care for the movie itself, praised its star, writing, "Christopher Reeve, the young actor chosen to play the lead in *Superman*, is the best reason to see the movie. He has an open-faced, deadpan style that's just right for a windup hero. Reeve plays innocent but not dumb, and the combination of his Pop jawline and physique with his unassuming manner makes him immediately likable."

"*Superman* is pure delight," wrote Roger Ebert, who liked the movie so much better than Kael that he rated it four stars in his *Chicago Tribune* review:

After a worldwide talent search to play the Man of Steel, they found the right guy. Christopher Reeve looks like the *Superman* in the comic books, but he's also an engaging actor, open and funny in his big love scene with Lois Lane, and then correctly awesome in his showdown with the arch-villain Lex Luthor. Reeve sells the role; wrong casting here would have sunk everything.

Despite the film's popularity and critical acclaim, *Superman* won only one Academy Award in 1979, for best visual effects. Reeve was not disappointed, however. Although he was not nominated for an Oscar, he won the Most Promising Newcomer award from the British equivalent of America's Motion Picture Academy.

Reeve did receive recognition of a sort at that year's Oscar presentations, though. Years later in an interview he recalled, "I was [backstage] standing next to John Wayne and Cary Grant, and heard Wayne tell him, 'This is our new man. He's taking over.' I thought, 'My God!' " [40]

A Reluctant Hero

Reeve's movie career was clearly on the rise, although he recognized the danger of taking too many roles similar to that of Superman. Not wanting to be typecast as a heroic figure in more action roles, Reeve turned down many such offers that included paychecks of a million dollars.

"After the success of *Superman,* one of my greatest problems as an actor was that my agents and many Hollywood producers wanted me to be an action hero, which didn't interest me," Reeve wrote. "My eyes glazed over with boredom when two producers and a studio executive once pitched the idea of my playing Eric the Red in an epic adventure about the Vikings. I could just imagine myself with an iron helmet and horns on my head."[41]

"I wanted to be an actor, not run around with a machine gun,"[42] Reeve told an interviewer. Additionally, he wrote in his autobiography:

> Sometimes, I got the sinking feeling that I had inadvertently closed the door to my future as a legitimate actor. I made it clear to everyone who worked with me that I was still interested in the theater and that I wanted to play parts that were complex and challenging. I told them I would rather be in a good film that might not make a lot of money than a lousy film that grossed a hundred million.

> Over the next few years, I discovered that *Superman* had actually opened many doors; the question was how to make the best use of these opportunities.[43]

Jane Seymour costarred with Reeve in the fantasy film Somewhere in Time.

Hoping to avoid being typecast as an action hero, Reeve chose an offbeat romantic drama for his first movie after *Superman.* He starred in the fantasy *Somewhere in Time*—for far less money and against the advice of his agent—because he liked the story and his role. He portrayed a young playwright who travels back in time to the early 1900s in order to romance a beautiful actress of the period, played by Jane Seymour.

Critics were not kind to the film or Reeve's performance, but many viewers liked him and the film's old-fashioned romance. Over the years *Somewhere in Time* has gained a large "cult" following. A worldwide fan club for the movie now boasts more than seven thousand members.

Superman Returns

At the same time *Superman —the Movie* was filmed, many scenes were also shot for a sequel. New scenes had to be added, however, and Reeve was not eager to don the cape and tights again, but his contract called for it, at a much higher salary than before.

Superman II, released in 1980, was also a big success with both critics and the public. Reeve later wrote, "I think *Superman II* may be the best of the series, because it has some effective comedy."[44]

Despite the sequel's success, Reeve drew greater acting satisfaction that year from appearing in plays at Williamstown, such as *The Cherry Orchard* and *The Front Page.* He then had a hit on Broadway. Starring in *The Fifth of July,* he was praised by critics for his portrayal of a Vietnam War amputee on crutches and in a wheelchair.

Reeve's next movie roles were varied. *Deathtrap,* costarring Michael Caine, was a murder mystery based on a successful stage play and was more a critical than a box-office success. Then he played an unscrupulous priest in *Monsignor,* which neither audiences nor critics liked.

A Second Life for *Somewhere in Time*

When even his successes in *The Bostonians* and *Remains of the Day* were not followed by better movie roles, Reeve found satisfaction in how important his second movie, *Somewhere in Time,* had become. The romantic fantasy had bombed when it was released fourteen years before but became a favorite of thousands of people when it was shown on videocassette or in revivals at art-movie houses or on college campuses. In October 1994, Reeve returned to Mackinac Island in Michigan's Upper Peninsula, where the movie had been filmed, to attend an annual meeting of fans of the picture, members of the International Network of *Somewhere in Time* Enthusiasts.

"The movie holds the prime place by the fireside in my heart," he told his fans. "This is the one that I have the greatest gratitude for. The fact that you've created such support for it moves me more than you ever can know."

Reeve with Margot Kidder in Superman II.

Reeve then returned to playing the Man of Steel in *Superman III*. Movie and television comic Richard Pryor was hired to play a comic villain, but the script writers then allowed him to dominate the film. Its switch of emphasis to more humor, some of it slapstick, made the film unsuccessful with critics and audiences. Reeve was also unhappy with the film, later writing: "[It was] a movie that became more of a Richard Pryor comedy vehicle than a proper Superman film."[45]

Searching for Identity as an Actor

Over the next ten years, Reeve seldom found movie roles that satisfied him as much as those he played onstage in New York, London, or when he returned frequently to the Williamstown Theater in Massachusetts. The stage became a refuge for him from the disappointments of his movie roles. He performed in thirteen stage productions at Williamstown between 1980 and 1994, for the low basic weekly salary of $225. His diverse roles ranged from Achilles in *The Greeks* to Morris Townsend, the handsome but insincere suitor in *The Heiress*.

Although he found satisfaction acting onstage, Reeve kept working in films. During this period he appeared in more than fifty movies, television films, and documentaries. Few of them were of much importance to him or got him much credit. A notable exception was a prestigious British film for which he got excellent reviews in 1984. In *The Bostonians*, from a novel by Henry James and set in 1875 Boston, Reeve costarred with famous actresses Vanessa Redgrave and Jessica Tandy. He played the part of a lawyer in love with an early participant in the feminist movement.

Critics praised Reeve for his performance in *The Bostonians*, but what pleased him even more was a telephone message he later received from Katharine Hepburn while he was in Hungary filming his next movie, *Anna Karenina*. He was told she said, "Tell him I'm calling to say he was absolutely marvelous in *The Bostonians*." [46]

Reeve had been offered a million dollars to star as Fletcher Christian in a remake of *Mutiny on the Bounty*, but turned it down to play in *The Bostonians* for only $120,000. Reeve did this because his role in the more intellectual period drama appealed more to the classical actor in him than did the role of a leader of mutineers. He also accepted a "bribe" from the film's coproducer, Ismail Merchant, in the form of a home-cooked Indian dinner once a week. When the filming finished, he presented Reeve with a T-shirt that read, "I did it for curry."

Despite being typecast earlier as an action hero, Reeve got the part in *The Bostonians* over the objections of some of the movie's backers, who thought he was not marketable in a serious, literate film. Reeve proved them wrong, and was so good that Redgrave got him hired to play opposite her on the London stage in another play based on a Henry James work, *The Aspern Papers*. He again got good notices for that performance.

But more disappointing film and television movie roles followed even those successes, and Reeve again found more satisfaction on the stage, in plays at Williamstown.

Despite his stage successes, Reeve still found that *Superman* haunted his career. Still more mediocre movie roles followed. The big-budgeted television movie *Anna Karenina*, based on the

Reeve achieved critical and popular success with his role in The Bostonians.

Tolstoy novel, was one of these. Reeve was happy working on location in Hungary, because *Superman* had never been shown there, so people accepted him without knowing of his cape-and-tights role. But *Anna Karenina* did not bring Reeve the critical praise he sought, although everyone agreed he looked very handsome in a Russian cavalry uniform and with a mustache as Count Vronsky.

Anna Karenina, however, would affect Reeve's life in ways he never dreamed. His allergy to horses caused him to sneeze, so he had done very little riding, but his role in the television movie called for him to be an accomplished horseman. Practicing with expert Hungarian horsemen, Reeve fell in love with the sport of cross-country horse jumping, even though he considered it the most dangerous thing he did. When he returned to the United States after completing the movie, he began entering horse-jumping competitions. Other changes in Reeve's life lay ahead as well.

A New Life

Reeve's and Gae Exton's romance had begun to cool by 1985. "I'm a romantic, a dreamer," he explained later. "Gae is a practical person. She's organized, focused in terms of common sense, always looking for the logic in things. I'm sometimes instinctive, impulsive. She's a consistent person, whereas I tend to be moody. I blow hot and cold."[47]

The couple separated early in 1987, but remained friends. Reeve often spent four months at a time with his children in England. He seemed to enjoy the role of father more than any other.

Besides spending time with his children, Reeve found satisfaction in what fame and wealth had bought him: an airplane, a glider, a yacht, and several homes, both in London and in California.

The summer after his separation from Gae Exton, Reeve's personal life took a very positive turn. One night after appearing in a play called *The Rover* at the Williamstown Theater, he joined some friends at a nearby cabaret. He immediately became interested in the young singer onstage. He thought Dana Morosini, with straight brown hair and soft brown eyes, was beautiful.

"She wore an off-the-shoulder dress and sang 'The Music That Makes Me Dance,'" Reeve recalled. "Right then I went down, hook, line, and sinker."[48] After she sang, Reeve went backstage and asked her to go with him to a party. She declined, however, having heard he was a ladies' man.

Dana's first response, she later told an interviewer, was "Here was this cheesecake Superman. I thought, if I was going to date an actor, I wanted a *real* actor. Of course, all you have to do is talk to him for ten minutes, and you see how intelligent and sensitive he is."[49]

Reeve persisted, and Dana later accepted his invitation to go out with him. Gradually their friendship grew into love. "It was a very old-fashioned courtship," Dana recalled. "He'd come over to watch me rehearse. He'd pick wildflowers and have them carried over by an apprentice."[50]

As their relationship deepened, Dana wanted them to marry. Reeve, however, was reluctant to commit himself to marriage because of his parents' divorce and the instability of his mother's

During his courtship of Dana Morosini, Reeve was forced to deal with his fear of commitment.

second marriage. "I saw marriage as a loss rather than a gain," he wrote later. "All my life I had heard people say that they loved each other and that they would be together forever, to have and to hold from this day forward, and so forth, and then it would turn out not to be true."[51]

Reeve eventually agreed to undergo counseling to get over his fear of marriage or of having a long, lasting relationship. In 1992, five years after he had met Dana, the therapy had helped Reeve to overcome those fears. He proposed to Dana over a candlelight dinner in his penthouse apartment in New York City and she accepted.

A son was born to the Reeves later in 1992. He was named William (nicknamed "Will"), after Reeve's love of the Williamstown Theater Festival.

Reeve was happy in his personal life, despite making four more disappointing television movies that year. He also costarred in a feature film, *Noises Off,* a comedy with Michael Caine and Carol Burnett, that did not enhance any of their careers.

A New Movie Success

While his career was stalled in disappointing roles, mainly in movies made for television, Reeve scored a big screen movie success in 1993 for a supporting role in one of the most impor-

tant movies of the year. *Remains of the Day,* another prestigious British film, starred Anthony Hopkins and Emma Thompson. In this film, Reeve played a rich American senator who buys the estate of an Englishman secretly working for the Germans in World War II. Critics praised his performance as his best movie work since *Superman.*

Reeve agreed, as he later said in an interview. "I'm proudest of my work in *Remains of the Day.* Even though it was a small part, it was my most natural performance."[52]

Reeve's role in Remains of the Day brought him critical praise after a disappointing series of films.

For Christopher Reeve in 1993, one year into his fourth decade, his movie career and personal life had taken a giant turn for the better. It looked like his best years lay ahead.

Chapter 4

The Actor as Activist

DESPITE A BUSY CAREER and private life during the years after achieving stardom in *Superman*, Christopher Reeve found time for a great deal of public service. Following his father's example, he became a social and political activist. His main cause was protecting the environment, but he also became active in helping the homeless, preserving funding for the arts, protesting creative censorship, and fund-raising for AIDS victims and research. He was active in helping needy children around the world, as spokesperson for Save the Children and fund-raising for Child Hope. He also risked his life to free persecuted actors and writers outside the United States.

A Crusader for the Environment and World Peace

As a lover of outdoor activities, such as flying, sailing, and skiing, Reeve became a champion of environmental causes. He contributed time and lent his prestige to campaigns to protect parks for recreation, preserve natural habitats for animals, and improve air and water quality.

After appearing onstage again in New York in 1985, this time in a nonmusical version of the opera *The Marriage of Figaro*, Reeve was offered three million dollars to star in a fourth Superman movie. Even though he did not want to play the action hero yet again, he agreed to don the tights and cape one more time on the condition that he could have a hand in its story. He wanted a screenplay in which Superman would crusade for world peace. The producers, fearful that a new Superman movie could not be a success without Reeve, agreed.

To further sweeten the pot, the producers offered Reeve an extra million dollars to make a movie of his own choice beforehand. The movie he chose to make was *Street Smart*, costarring Morgan Freeman. Reeve's character was unsavory, and critics and the public did not find him believable. The reaction was probably due to the fact that his role was too far removed from the image they still had of him as a clean-cut hero.

Discouraged with his movie career, and not looking forward to playing Superman again, Reeve threw his energies into environmental causes.

Reeve the Environmentalist

Reeve became a board member of the Charles Lindbergh Fund, which provides grants for environmentally sound new technologies. He also lent his support to causes of the Natural Resources Defense Council. He joined the Environmental Air Force, using his seven-seat airplane to fly government officials and journalists to see where lumber companies had cut down hundreds of acres of trees in Maine forests and then left the area environmentally damaged.

Protecting the environment also led Reeve to become active in politics for the first time in his life, when he campaigned in 1986 for the reelection of U.S. senator Patrick Leahy, a liberal Vermont environmentalist. Reeve attracted an enthusiastic crowd when he flew his plane into Burlington for a Leahy rally, and his endorsement helped Leahy easily win reelection.

Reeve then contributed ideas to a screenplay for the fourth Superman movie, *Superman IV: The Quest for Peace*. It conveyed a strong message on behalf of world peace.

"We're living in a global village now," Reeve explained to an interviewer about the theme of the movie, "and there has to be a new heightened awareness of our interactions as people on this planet. I hope for a new age in the next century where we begin to take responsibility for this planet as a whole rather than our particular little horizon right in front of us."[53]

At the end of the movie, Superman gathers all the world's nuclear weapons and hurls them into the sun. Then he lectures the United Nations on world peace.

To his dismay, Reeve found that even a superhuman effort was not enough to save Superman IV. *(Here, Gene Hackman and Reeve).*

Critics and audiences found that the message of *Superman IV* was too strong. However, there were other reasons it failed, some of which Reeve foresaw. Shortly before its release in 1987, Reeve had told Jon Cryer, a supporting actor in the film, that it was going to be "terrible."[54]

"The movie was his [Chris's] idea and the idea was great," Cryer later told an interviewer. "And then Cannon [the producers] ran out of money five months ahead of time and released an unfinished movie. That's why Chris leveled with me and said, 'It's a mess.'"[55]

Reeve later wrote that the movie was hampered by budget constraints, and the producers had nearly thirty projects in the works at the time, so his film received no special consideration. "*Superman IV* was simply a catastrophe from start to finish," he wrote. "That failure was a huge blow to my career."[56]

He worried that people might think he compromised his integrity by making a fourth Superman movie, since he often had said he did not want to don the cape again. "I just hope people aren't going to assume that I did the fourth one for big bucks, that I sold out, because that's not true," he told a reporter. "I needed the motivation to really want to play Superman again."[57] Having the Man of Steel crusade for world peace provided that motivation.

Reeve then found more satisfaction in returning to the stage in Williamstown and again focusing on environmental causes.

In 1990, Reeve narrated a television documentary, *Black Tide*, about the devastating *Exxon Valdez* oil tanker spill off the coast of Alaska. The accident killed wildlife and damaged the sensitive environment of Prince William Sound.

Reeve then lobbied in Washington in support of the Clean Air Act, which would monitor interstate and international air and water pollution and enforce cleaner and safer environmental standards. The act, which would also regulate acid rain and ozone pollution and require cleaner fuels for cars, trucks, and buses, later passed and became law that year.

In 1992, Reeve returned to politics when he worked for Bill Clinton's first presidential campaign, supporting his candidacy partly because of Clinton's support for the National Endowment for the Arts. He was also motivated by vice presidential candidate Al Gore's positions regarding protection of the environment.

Reeve continued his efforts on behalf of the environment in 1994 by narrating a public television documentary on saving gray whales. In "Gray Whales with Christopher Reeve," part of a series called *In the Wild*, Reeve explored the behavior of the whales during their migration from the Arctic off the coast of

Is Activism Risky for an Actor?

During an interview on CNN's *Larry King Live*, on April 3, 1990, King asked Reeve if he was taking a risk by being so outspoken (as an activist) and whether he might make people dislike him who ordinarily might attend his films. Reeve, who earlier in the day had lobbied for the federal Clean Air Act, replied,

> Well, people who aren't going to like me aren't going to like me anyway. . . . Life is not a popularity contest. The better off you are and the older I get, the more confident I get in just sticking to what I believe in, making sure that I'm fair, rational, and informed, and then saying what's on my mind. . . . I really do take the time to do my homework so that I'll have a certain credibility.

Siberia to the shores of Baja California. When his dream of coming face to face with a mother and its calf came true off Baja, Reeve called the trip "the adventure of a lifetime."[58]

Reeve also served as host of a Travel Channel television series, *Earth Journeys with Christopher Reeve*, that aired from 1994 to 1996. He was nominated twice for Cable ACE awards as best host for his work in the series of half-hour shows, which drew attention to environmental concerns around the world.

A Citizen Hero

Reeve was not afraid to take stands that might be unpopular, but on November 22, 1987, he was at his country house in Williamstown, Massachusetts, when he received a telephone call that greatly challenged his courage. A Chilean novelist and playwright, Ariel Dorfman, told him that seventy-seven of that country's top actors, directors, and playwrights would be sentenced to death by the dictator Augusto Pinochet if they refused to leave their country by the end of the month. Their crime was having criticized his regime in their theatrical works.

Dorfman sought "Superman's" help, asking Reeve to go to Chile and lead a rally to save his countrymen's lives. Reeve's prestige, Dorfman hoped, would draw international attention to their plight. The danger for Reeve was real; once on Chilean soil, he would himself be subject to arrest. He would make the trip with no official endorsement or protection from the U.S. government.

Knowing he might be risking his life, Reeve agreed to go. "It didn't require much soul-searching," he later told a reporter. "I couldn't think of anything coming up for me more important than that."[59]

Eight days later, Reeve flew to Santiago, Chile's capital, arriving only twenty-four hours before the actors and writers were due to be executed. They had continued to refuse to leave their country, and demonstrations were under way. Reeve saw young actors courageously walking the tear-gas-filled streets wearing T-shirts with red bull's-eyes and the words "Shoot me first."

Reeve met with the condemned artists, and one actor said his phone calls had been interrupted by bursts of machine-gun fire. Reeve knew then what a dangerous mission he had undertaken.

Reeve was to speak at a rally to be held in a sports stadium in one of the city's poorer sections at eight o'clock that night. When crowds of protesters filled the stands three hours before the rally was to begin, police declared it canceled. Three hundred troops with machine guns cordoned off the area.

Since the protesters were used to their meetings being called off by police, they had a backup plan. The rally was moved to a midtown garage that Reeve said later looked like a "rusty airplane hangar."[60] Several thousand people jammed into the dilapidated structure. "The atmosphere had become more highly charged," Reeve recalled. "The actors were angry now."[61]

Reeve was amazed by the reception he got when he entered the garage. People were screaming, stomping their feet, and tearing at his clothes. He had not even generated that much excitement when he made appearances dressed as Superman. "It was unbelievable," Reeve said later. "The kind of reception I associate with the Pope, or maybe the Beatles."[62]

As Reeve mounted a makeshift stage, the crowds began singing the song of their movement, "He [Pinochet] Will Fall." Then the lights went out. No one knew for certain why, and an anxious half an hour passed before lighting was restored.

There was no microphone, so Reeve spoke to the crowd in a loud stage voice. He did not speak Spanish, but read in that language from a letter he held up to show them. It was signed by movie stars Gene Hackman, Cher, Martin Sheen, Susan Sarandon, and Mia Farrow, asking that Pinochet free the imprisoned actors and writers.

Reeve then spoke in English, thanking the crowd for "this amazing day." He said he looked forward to returning to the United States "and telling them [Americans] what a brave and beautiful people you are."[63]

After his speech, a singer strummed a guitar and sang a revolutionary song as Reeve was cheered upon leaving. He returned to the United States the next day and learned from Dorfman that his daring effort had worked. Pinochet canceled his execution order. When Reeve's heroism was reported in the press, many credited him with saving the lives of his fellow actors and artists.

Reeve was more humble about his role in the drama. "This was not Superman to the rescue," he said. "It was me as a private citizen, and as an actor in a country where we take the freedom to perform for granted, helping fellow professionals in a country where they do not."[64]

Dorfman also saw something else in Reeve's heroism. "Chris is an example of how one can relate his art to his life," he said. "Chileans can never be thankful enough for his presence there that day."[65]

Several months later, in the face of escalating protests, Pinochet resigned. Reeve was later given two awards for bravery from the Walter Briehl Human Rights Foundation, a group that works with torture victims.

Reeve was asked if he would volunteer his services again on behalf of other artists suffering from political oppression, even if it meant risking his life. "Yes," he replied. "Of course."[66]

Chile's president Augusto Pinochet threatened to stifle the nation's creative freedom.

The Creative Coalition

Reeve increasingly saw the potential influence creative people could exert, if they were aware of issues and worked together. In 1990 he joined several other actors in forming the Creative Coalition (TCC), an organization to help celebrities speak knowledgeably on social issues. Other founders were actors Alec Baldwin, Susan Sarandon, Ron Silver, and Blythe Danner. Within months, hundreds of writers, stagehands, agents, publicists, and opera singers joined. Reeve eventually became the group's copresident.

In March 1995, Reeve addressed members of Congress during a breakfast meeting, telling them about the Creative Coalition and its goal to have an informed voice in social concerns. In his speech, referring to continued government support for the National Endowment for the Arts, he said, "There is a crucial role for the government to play in developing the arts and culture in this country." [67]

Reeve's social activism work did not go unnoticed. At his twentieth Princeton Country Day School reunion in 1990, he

Defending Creative Freedom

The Creative Coalition, which Christopher Reeve helped organize among actors and other artists, made its initial effort the defense of government funding for the arts, as he explained in *Still Me:*

> Our first major undertaking was to defend the National Endowment for the Arts [NEA] against attacks by conservative Republicans who were outraged that taxpayer dollars were being used to fund art they considered obscene.

> We argued successfully that in its twenty-five-year history the NEA had given over 90,000 grants and only about a dozen had ever provoked any controversy. Considering the cultural and economic benefit to the country and the provisions of the First Amendment [freedom of speech], we felt this was a small price to pay.

> It was also our contention that politicians do not have the right to impose content restrictions on federally funded art.

> Congress agreed. The NEA retained its government funding in 1990, although the issue has remained a source of controversy.

As copresident of the Creative Coalition, Reeve (second from right) attends a Congressional hearing on arts funding in February 1995.

received his class's Alumni Award. The recognition was not for his success as a movie star but for his volunteer work with some thirty charitable causes.

In giving Reeve the award, the school's headmaster, Duncan Alling, told the audience,

> He has given his time, his energy, and his mind to human rights activities in places like Chile. He has gone into hospitals and spent time with young people and old people who are in great pain. He has worked for other types of volunteer and charity organizations—whether it's supporting them through his voice and his presence in terms of advertising or giving his own time to these people.[68]

The reason he won the award pleased Reeve very much. He said the day made him "pleasantly embarrassed."[69]

Chapter 5

A Near-Fatal Accident

CHRISTOPHER REEVE NEARLY LOST his life in May 1995, when he fell from his horse in a jumping competition. After he landed on his head, the uppermost vertebrae in his spine were fractured. He was instantly paralyzed from the neck down. Even his diaphragm was paralyzed and he was unable to breathe. His life hung in the balance until doctors were able to literally reattach his head to his spine, but it was doubtful he would ever walk again.

A Dangerous Ride

Christopher Reeve, a very active person, had constantly challenged himself, not only in acting but in many sports and activities. Like his father, he wanted not only to be accomplished in many different areas but also the best in everything he tried.

There were few activities that Reeve considered beyond him. After becoming an expert sailor, scuba diver, tennis player, skier, and pilot (several times he flew solo across the Atlantic in a small plane), Reeve added horse jumping to his passions.

Of all his activities, it was jumping on horseback that presented the most hazards.

By his own admission, Reeve is someone who thrives on action. "I run on high-test gas," he told a reporter in 1979. "I'm over-energetic, a live wire." [70]

Playing hard and participating in dangerous pastimes presents special problems for movie stars. Movies cost many millions of dollars to make, and investors cannot risk their star being injured or killed in an accident. Because his taste for dangerous hobbies was well known, producers often insisted upon a "no flying during filming" clause in Reeve's contracts. As his new passion became known, a "no horse jumping" clause was added. Reeve always complied, and did again in 1994 during filming of *Above Suspicion.* In this movie made for cable television he played the part of a paralyzed police officer confined to a wheelchair. Once filming was completed, he resumed horse jumping.

Early in 1995, Reeve bought a thoroughbred chestnut gelding that was said to be fearless in both stadium and cross-country jumping. He named the horse Buck, and he began practicing so he could enter horse-jumping competitions. Aware that head injuries are a real danger to equestrians, he volunteered his free services to pose for a poster for the American Medical Equestrian Association to promote the practice of wearing a helmet while engaging in horseback riding. He also narrated a 4-H Club video on head-injury prevention. The irony of these activities would soon become apparent.

Reeve's next movie was to be *Kidnapped,* a family film based on the Robert Louis Stevenson adventure novel, which was to be filmed in Ireland. Before starting work on the movie, he planned to compete in a major equestrian competition in Virginia.

On Memorial Day weekend, Saturday, May 27, Reeve drove with his wife and their three-year-old son, Will, from their home in Bedford, New York, to Culpeper County, Virginia, near

Reeve makes a jump in a cross-country event at the King Oak Farm Horse Trials in Southampton, Massachusetts, on May 14, 1995.

Washington, D.C. There he entered the spring horse trials of the Commonwealth Dressage and Combined Training Association.

Reeve was forty-two and in great physical condition, standing six feet four inches tall and weighing a trim 215 pounds. He seemed happy and at ease, about to ride in one of the cross-country jumping events on the bright, hot, and humid day.

Although cross-country horse jumping may look graceful and effortless, it is actually a physically and mentally demanding exercise in control. Timing and balance are essential in riding a twelve-hundred-pound animal over a fence or stone wall. Jumping requires lots of practice. Wanting to be better than just "good," Reeve often practiced horse jumping several hours a day.

On the morning of the race day, to familiarize himself and his horse with the jumps, Reeve walked Buck around the course four times, twice what most other riders would do. Before competing that afternoon, he led Buck around the course once more, then got dressed in his blue-and-silver silk riding shirt, off-white breeches, protective vest, knee-high boots, and helmet.

Reeve and his horse began a fifteen-hurdle, two-mile cross-country course. His rhythm was fine, and he cleared the first two hurdles without any problem.

The third jump was a zigzag log fence only three feet three inches high. Reeve and his horse were galloping easily toward the jump. His approach was good. Reeve leaned over the neck of his horse, to take the jump.

Reeve later told what happened next:

Buck started to jump the fence, but all of a sudden he just put on the brakes. No warning, no hesitation, no sense of anything wrong.

He just stopped. It was what riders call a dirty stop; it occurs without warning. Someone said a rabbit ran out and spooked Buck. Someone said it could have been shadows. . . .

When I went over, I took the bridle, the bit, the reins, everything off Buck's face. I landed right on my head because my hands were entangled in the bridle and I couldn't get an arm free to break my fall.

I flipped over, landing on the other side of the fence.[71]

"Superman" Becomes Paralyzed

An organizer of the horse trials, Helmut Boehme, was nearby and rushed to Reeve as the competition stopped. He saw that Reeve was lying on the turf motionless, unconscious and apparently not breathing, his lips turning blue. "The life had gone out of him,"[72] Boehme said later in an interview.

An anesthesiologist who by amazing good fortune also happened to be nearby, then saved Reeve's life. She gave him mouth-to-mouth resuscitation until paramedics at the park could arrive. Reeve was very lucky that this doctor, whose identity was never revealed, had gotten him breathing again so soon, since after four minutes of not breathing, brain damage begins.

A "Fluke" Creates a Nightmare

Ironically, and what few people know, Reeve had at first not planned to compete in the equestrian event at Culpeper, Virginia, as he wrote in his autobiography:

> The fact that I went to Culpeper at all was a fluke. I had originally signed up to compete that weekend at an event in Vermont. I'd had success in Vermont the year before. I'd finished first in one event at Tamarack and placed third in [another]. I'd met a lot of nice people. I also preferred the cool weather. I figured that on Memorial Day weekend, it would be more pleasant in Vermont than down in Virginia.

Reeve said he was influenced to enter the Culpeper event by horsemen friends at a stable near Bedford, owned by Bill McGuinness, where he had moved his horse about a month before.

> Most of the barns in the area concentrate on dressage or hunters or jumpers, but Bill ran the only combined training barn and had a group of half a dozen loyal clients, all of whom were as motivated as I was. They had decided to go to Culpeper for the Memorial Day weekend, and Bill invited me to come along. I knew from experience that it's more fun to compete as a group, so I agreed to go and got an entry in at the last minute. I've since learned that this sort of impulsive decision is [typically a factor in] many accidents.

> I've often thought that if I'd stuck to the original plan nothing bad would have happened. But Dana pointed out that if we'd gone sailing that weekend instead, I could just as easily have been hit in the head by the boom, knocked overboard, and drowned. An accident can happen at any time, even to someone who is cautious and in control.

Reeve later wrote about what the paramedics did: "They stabilized my head and managed to keep me alive by squeezing air into my body with an ambu bag. They managed to hold my head still enough to put on a collar that immobilized my neck."[73]

Medics then transported Reeve by ambulance to nearby Culpeper Medical Center. Three doctors examined him and agreed he had shattered the first and second cervical vertebrae, those closest to the skull. Reeve's injuries were clearly life threatening. In his fall from the horse he had damaged his spinal cord, through which twenty million nerve fibers run up and down the center of the spine, carrying impulses between the brain and the rest of the body. "This is called a hangman's injury," Reeve later wrote, "because it's the kind of break that happens when the trapdoor opens and the noose snaps tight [around a person's neck]."[74]

Reeve's wife and son were not at the event when he fell, but were at a nearby hotel awaiting his return. Dana was always present when Reeve competed in equestrian events, often videotaping near the most difficult jumps. But on this particular occasion, she was back at the hotel, where Will was taking a nap. Informed by telephone of the accident, Dana woke the boy and rushed with him to the medical center. Upon arriving, they found paramedics preparing to transfer Reeve by helicopter to the University of Virginia Medical Center, where more specialized care was available. Before takeoff, medics suggested Dana say good-bye to her husband, in case he did not survive the flight.

Less than an hour after his fall, Reeve was flown to the medical center, about forty-five miles away in Charlottesville. There he would receive some of the finest care possible from doctors experienced in treating vertebrae and spinal cord injuries. Despite the excellent medical care, Reeve's injuries were serious and the outlook uncertain.

As news of Reeve's accident spread, the world knew what had happened to Superman long before the actor who played him did. Reeve awoke four days later to learn he was a quadriplegic. Paralyzed from the neck down, he was unable to move his arms or legs or to breathe without the use of a respirator.

Reeve's injury caused spinal cord inflammation that steadily destroyed the essential functions of his body: breathing, bladder and bowel control, and any motion below the neck. His heart continued to function normally, however, and there was one other bit of good news: he had not suffered brain damage.

The Will to Live

As he lay helpless in the hospital, Reeve's family hurried to his bedside. Dana and Will were the first to arrive, soon followed by his mother, father, stepfather, and brother. His former lover Gae Exton and their son, Matthew, fifteen, and daughter Alexandra, eleven, also came right away from London.

As the extensiveness of his injury became clear to him, the thought of spending the rest of his life paralyzed and in a wheelchair made Reeve contemplate suicide. He also did not want to

Among those who rushed to be with the injured Reeve were his daughter, Alexandra; Gae Exton; and his son, Matthew.

be a burden to those he loved and who would have to take care
of him. Reeve asked Dana if she still wanted him the way he was
now. Or maybe they should let him go. Reeve wrote in *Still Me*
what her tearful response was:

> She said, "I am only going to say this once: I will support
> whatever you want to do, because this is your life, and
> your decision. But I want you to know that I'll be with
> you for the long haul, no matter what. . . .
>
> Then she added the words that saved my life: "You're
> still you. And I love you."[75]

Dana's words were a kind of revelation to someone who had
yearned for so long to feel part of a family, as Reeve later wrote:

> It meant more to me than just a personal declaration of
> faith and commitment. In a sense, it was an affirmation
> that marriage and family stood at the center of every-
> thing, and if both were intact, so was your universe.
> Many people have known this all their lives. I did not.[76]

Later, in a television interview with Barbara Walters, Dana
Reeve told viewers that physical abilities are not what matter:

> When it's actually the person you love, the person you
> know and there's no head injury, no brain damage, it's him,
> it's the essence of him, and that's what I said to him. . . . I
> also said, though, of course, that it was his decision, but that
> I would be here for the long run—no matter what, no mat-
> ter what had happened, I would be there.[77]

His wife's love and devotion, and the sight of his three children coming into his room, gave Reeve the courage to live and
face whatever his future might hold.

Reeve told Walters in the same interview,

> I could see how much they needed me and wanted me.
> What happens to me when I have a problem is I get em-
> barrassed. I go like, oh, I don't want to cause you people
> trouble, and I don't want people to be burdened to take
> care of me, you know?

Dana Reeve poses with her paralyzed husband in November 1995.

That was my thought briefly on that afternoon, and the minute they all came in and I could see the love and feel the love and know that we're still a family . . . the thought [of suicide] vanished, and it has never come back again.[78]

A Fifty-Fifty Operation

Because of the shattered vertebrae, Reeve's head was virtually separated from his body, held in place only by muscle and other soft tissue. Doctors would have to reconstruct the shattered pieces of his spine. The procedure would be difficult, and Reeve's chance of surviving it were no better than fifty-fifty. Dr. John A. Jane, one of the nation's leading neurosurgeons, would perform the delicate operation. He was encouraged because although Reeve's spinal cord had been damaged, it was not completely severed.

On June 5, nine days after Reeve's fall, when his vital signs had sufficiently stabilized, Dr. Jane led a team of doctors who performed a six-and-a-half-hour operation securing Reeve's head to his spine. Reeve later wrote how this was done:

Laughter Is the Best Medicine

Nine days after his fall, Reeve was to undergo major surgery to reattach his neck to his spine. The prospect frightened him, as he revealed
in his autobiography:

> As the day of the operation drew closer, it became more and
> more painful and frightening to contemplate. In spite of efforts
> to protect me from the truth, I already knew that I had only a
> fifty-fifty chance of surviving the surgery.
>
> I lay on my back, frozen, unable to avoid thinking the darkest
> thoughts. Then, at an especially bleak moment, the door flew
> open and in hurried a squat fellow with a blue scrub hat and a
> yellow surgical gown and glasses, speaking in a Russian accent.
> He announced that he was my proctologist [a specialist in disor-
> der of the rectum] and that he had to examine me immediately.
>
> My first reaction was that either I was on way too many drugs or
> I was in fact brain damaged. But it was Robin Williams. He and
> his wife, Marsha, had materialized from who knows where. And
> for the first time since the accident, I laughed. My old friend had
> helped me know that somehow I was going to be okay.

At the time I had no idea that the kind of surgery they
would perform on me had never been done before. Dr.
Jane had to reattach my head to my spinal column without causing brain damage while giving me the possibil-
ity of movement.

He placed wires under both laminae—the bony cover-
ings of the spinal cord. He took bone from my hip and
squeezed it down to get a solid fit between C1 and C2
[the top two cervical vertebrae]. Then he put in a titanium pin the shape of a small croquet wicket and fused
the sublaminal wires with the first and second vertebrae.
Finally, he drilled holes in my skull and passed the wires
through to get a solid fusion.

What Jane did, in short, was put my head back on my
body.[79]

The operation was a success and gave Reeve's skull a firm
attachment to his neck. Reeve was appropriately grateful, telling
Jane about a year later, "You performed a miracle. I want to
thank you for giving me my life."[80]

But Reeve would never forget the complexity and danger of the operation, as he wrote later: "I'm glad I didn't know ahead of time what they were doing. As they wired the titanium pin in place, time and time again their tools came within a sixteenth of an inch of the brain stem. But they operated flawlessly. I can hardly believe what they accomplished."[81]

After the operation, Reeve began a long recovery process. He would be supported in that effort by his family, friends, and fans.

Friends and Fans Rally to Reeve

In the weeks following his accident and operation, some four hundred thousand letters and get-well cards arrived for Reeve from all over the world. Other well-wishers, including President Bill Clinton and Katharine Hepburn, telephoned. He also received more than two hundred bouquets of flowers, children's drawings, books, videos, posters, and pledges of prayers from friends, fans, movie and theater colleagues, as well as from other spinal cord injury victims.

In the mail was a picture postcard someone he did not know had sent him of the pyramid of Quetzalcoatl, a Mayan temple in Mexico with hundreds of steps leading up to a blue sky. Reeve had the picture taped to the bottom of the vital signs monitor over his bed so he could see it often. "I let it become a metaphor for the future," Reeve said in his autobiography. "I began to imagine myself climbing those steps, one at a time, until finally I would reach the top."[82]

Reeve could not feel it, but each day his wife clasped his hands lovingly. She would cheer him by singing "This Pretty Planet," a song they both had often sung to their son. These visits from Dana, he believes, helped him the most. For him, she was "medication—better than any drug they ever gave me."[83]

The Process of Rehabilitation Begins

After a month of care at the Virginia Medical Center, on June 28 Reeve was moved to the Kessler Institute, in New Jersey, where he began rehabilitation. Besides medical specialists attending him, there was a team of therapists—physical, speech, occupational, vocational, recreational, and respiratory.

Reeve's Way Out

In *Still Me*, Reeve described how he found the courage to live and to face the long years of rehabilitation that he became confident would one day lead him to walk again.

> When a catastrophe happens, it's easy to feel so sorry for yourself that you can't even see anybody around you. But the way out is through your relationships.

> The way out of that misery or obsession is to focus more on what your boy needs or what your teenagers need, or what other people around you need. It's very hard to do, and often you have to force yourself. But that is the answer to the dilemma of being frozen—at least it's the answer I found.

Reeve began getting four hours of therapy a day, and the routine included a series of neck exercises and stretching his legs and arms to prevent the tendons and muscles from shrinking. He also got an aerobic workout on a Regis Cycle, a device that forced his legs to move progressively faster.

After several weeks, Reeve was able to spend part of his days in a forty thousand dollar electric wheelchair equipped with controls that could be worked by sucking air into or blowing air out of a pipe. He could sit upright in the wheelchair because his head was held immobile in a brace, to protect it from spasms. Before long, he was able to move his head from side to side, chew his food, and even shrug his shoulders. He was also learning how to speak again by controlling the respirator that helped him to breathe.

Shortly after Reeve had arrived at Kessler, Dana had hung a poster in his room. It was a huge photograph of the space shuttle taking off from Cape Kennedy, Florida. America's astronauts had autographed the poster and at the bottom was the message, "We found nothing is impossible."[84]

Encouraged by the astronauts, Reeve told his new doctor, Marcalee Sipski, a spinal-cord specialist, that he wanted to be "proactive" in his recovery efforts. "I believe I'm going to walk again."[85]

Reeve repeated this assertion in a television interview with Katie Couric on NBC's *Today Show*. He said that his wife and children provided the motivation he needed to recover. "Without Dana, I couldn't do any of this. Without my kids, I couldn't do any of this. They're my reason to push and to keep going." [86]

Reeve's progress was good, but he still was not out of the woods. One day, his heart stopped because of an allergic reaction he had to an experimental drug he had been given. He was rushed to Saint Barnabas Hospital in nearby Livingston, New Jersey, where medics stabilized his condition.

By the end of July, he was still using a respirator to breathe, but at least he could speak clearly. He had learned to speak using the air he exhaled from his ventilator, which forces air into his lungs through a tracheotomy tube inserted in his neck. Gradually, over a period of months, he learned to breathe without the respirator, but it was a long, painful, and often frightening process.

Meanwhile, Reeve mastered a computer that understood verbal commands, enabling him to send e-mail and fax messages to friends. Besides faxing jokes to Robin Williams, he began badgering his agents on what work he could look forward

For Reeve, the courage to face fear came from the strength of his relationship with his wife, Dana, and his family. Reeve is shown here with Dana and son Will in 1997.

to. But it was not always possible for him to keep his spirits up. He continued to rely on his family to give him hope.

Home Again

Doctors at Kessler encouraged Reeve by promising that he could be home before Christmas, to continue rehabilitation at his house in Bedford, New York. While Dana waited for his homecoming, she hired carpenters to widen doors and install ramps to accommodate his wheelchair. At first it seemed that it would cost too much to have an elevator installed, so he would only be able to use the house's first floor. Later, however, the elevator was installed so he could go upstairs. The garage was converted into a gym he could use, with special exercise equipment designed for use by victims of paralysis.

Before leaving the rehabilitation center, Reeve demonstrated his determination to survive his paralysis by thanking the staff at Kessler for having "set the stage for my continued recovery."[87]

He said he had a lot to thank them for. He was leaving with some sensation of life in his left leg and right arm, as well as along his spine. He could breathe for fifteen minutes without the ventilator, and his diaphragm was getting stronger because of his daily breathing exercises.

It had taken Reeve every ounce of energy and determination he could summon, but his rehabilitation efforts at Kessler had paid off. He knew he still had a long way to go, but he would make the journey one step at a time. He had already taken the first steps, at Kessler. On December 13, he was finally back home, to do whatever it would take to make his dream come true. One day, he was determined, he would walk again.

Chapter 6

Activist in a Wheelchair

WHILE IN REHABILITATION following his accident, Christopher Reeve gained inner strength from realizing his productive life need not be over even though he was a quadriplegic. Others in his condition had not given up. Why should he? Summoning amazing courage, he made up his mind that if he might never make another movie or appear on the stage again, his life could still have meaning if he continued his activism, this time from a wheelchair.

A New Purpose in Life

About 250,000 Americans suffer from paralysis due to spinal cord injuries. Some 10,000 such injuries happen each year from sports such as horseback riding, diving, motorcycling, or from other accidents.

Reeve learned that if the brain is not damaged, as it fortunately was not in his case, many who are paralyzed can lead happy and successful lives. The active man who had played Superman in four movies, and in real life always faced up to a challenge, now faced being confined to a wheelchair, perhaps for the rest of his life. But he became determined that he would be a quadriplegic who would survive.

In the long hours alone with his thoughts at the Kessler Institute, Reeve thought about his accident and what meaning it had for him. He decided that it had not happened for a reason, but he still wondered if a purpose might come out of his becoming paralyzed. "Things happen fairly randomly," Reeve said in a radio

"This Is What Fun Is"

Christopher Reeve's prestige and story of personal courage make him a natural choice when an occasion demands an inspirational speaker. In his address to graduates of the University of Virginia on May 16, 1998, he challenged his listeners with this definition of fun:

> Fun is not about partying or just enjoying life or relaxing into a kind of complacency. Fun is about hard work and the rewards that come with it.
>
> It's about picking something that may be difficult, that'll challenge you, that requires self-discipline, that'll sometimes make you angry and frustrated. But if you pull through all that, that's fun.

interview several years later when he reflected on what his accident meant to him.

> The challenge is after an injury like this, after a life-changing experience, to discover meaning, finding a way of putting it into perspective.
>
> My challenge as I recovered was not only to recover my body, but to recover a sense of purpose, and fortunately I have been able to do that.[88]

While Reeve continued undergoing therapy toward achieving his goal of walking again, he began to think of ways he could turn his misfortune into something that could help others, as well as himself. His new purpose in life would be to help find a cure for paralysis.

A Whirlwind of Activity

Reeve began his campaign to help spinal cord injury victims by joining with philanthropist and fellow equestrian Joan Irvine Smith in establishing the Reeve-Irvine Research Center at the University of California at Irvine in January 1996. The multimillion-dollar facility is dedicated to spinal cord injury (SCI) research.

"The reason she wanted to start this foundation was because I didn't blame my horse [for the fall]," Reeve told CNN's Larry King. He added that after the accident, Buck was sold to "a young lady north of Boston [who] is riding him and doing very well."[89]

In an effort to directly aid victims of spinal cord injury, Reeve then began lobbying for federal legislation to increase the cap insurance companies place on policyholders' lifetime claims for catastrophic illnesses from $1 million to $10 million. His own policy had a cap of $1.2 million and his annual medical costs were $400,000, meaning that even his considerable financial resources would eventually be exhausted. He appeared on national television to promote the measure, but the U.S. Senate rejected it. Undeterred, Reeve continued to lobby for the higher insurance caps.

Reeve recognized that raising insurance payments is not the whole solution. When in 1996 a reporter for *Good Housekeeping* magazine asked what he hoped to accomplish in his activism on behalf of SCI victims, Reeve replied that money needed to be spent not just caring for the injured, but on developing cures.

I hope that with a groundswell of public support we can convince Washington to spend more money on research to cure people with spinal cord injuries, rather than just take care of them. Each year the federal government

Reeve's activist spirit remains undaunted as he continues to campaign for social causes. Here Reeve speaks at a press conference at a rehabilitation center in 1996.

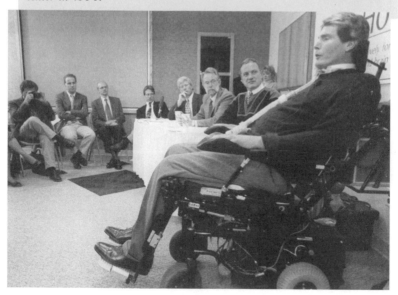

spends billions of dollars on Medicaid and Medicare payments to Americans who suffer neurological afflictions, including spinal cord injuries. This does nothing to improve them; it just keeps them ticking.

An increased investment in research to prevent and cure these conditions would radically reduce the costs to both the public and private sectors, now estimated at $8.7 billion a year.

Scientists project that if they spent another $40 million a year on research over the next decade, there would be significant improvements. If we can convince Congress that they should fix people like me, they could save billions on Medicaid and Medicare.[90]

Reeve explained that the federal government, in trying to save money on payments to disabled people, was on the wrong track. In an interview with Roger Rosenblatt for *Time* magazine he explained,

The way to save the Medicare-Medicaid issue, the way to turn it around, instead of talking about [benefit] cuts, is to talk about research and the efficacy of research. Because you won't have to pay to maintain injured people. We get things done in this country based on incentives, not just the goodness of our hearts.[91]

Reeve also pointed out that SCI research also benefits related diseases, such as multiple sclerosis, Parkinson's disease, Alzheimer's, Lou Gehrig's disease, and stroke.

In an attempt to bring his personal prestige to bear on behalf of paralysis victims, in 1996 Reeve became a member of the board of directors of the American Paralysis Association (APA), which funds SCI research, and later its chairman. He also became president of the Christopher Reeve Foundation, which raises money for the APA and also supplies to paralysis victims necessary equipment and services that are not covered by their insurance.

In addition, in March of that year Reeve made a taped appearance on national television telling of his admiration for the

athletes with disabilities who would be participating in the
Paralympics as part of the 1996 Olympic Games.

As Reeve's own recovery progressed, he offered himself as
an inspiration to other victims of spinal cord injury. That spring,
he made a wheelchair appearance in Green Springs, Ohio, to
christen an $18 million wing of the St. Francis Health Care
Centre for spinal cord injuries. "You can do anything you think
you can,"[92] he told patients there.

Continuing his fund-raising efforts, Reeve traveled to
Washington, D.C., in May to host a reception for the Dana Alliance
for Brain Initiatives, a group raising funds for SCI research. He then
met with President Bill Clinton and other federal officials to lobby
for money for SCI research. He said he was sure that with enough
funding for SCI research, thousands of paralyzed people could be
helped and that he would be able to walk in seven years, in time for
his fiftieth birthday. Clinton pledged to allocate $10 million to the
National Institutes of Health for SCI research.

*Reeve discusses his efforts to lobby Congress for increased funding for
spinal cord injury research at a news conference on Capitol Hill in 1996.*

Reeve Speaks at Oscar Ceremonies

Reeve believes that the American film industry has a role to play in raising awareness of social problems of the day. One of the first things Reeve did when he returned to activism after his accident was to attend the 68th Academy Awards presentations in Los Angeles on March 21, 1996. He had something important he wanted to tell the movie industry.

After a thousand of his Hollywood friends gave tuxedo-clad Reeve a standing ovation as he sat onstage in his respirator-equipped wheelchair, he joked,

> What you probably don't know is I left New York last September and I just arrived here this morning. And I'm glad I did because I wouldn't have missed this kind of welcome for the world. Thank you.

Reeve then introduced a short film, *Hollywood Tackles the Issues*, with scenes from past and recent movies that put social issues ahead of box-office success. They included *The Grapes of Wrath*, a 1940 film about the plight of migrant workers in the 1930s Great Depression; *Coming Home* (1978), about a paraplegic Vietnam War veteran; *Schindler's List* (1993), about persecution of Jews in World War II; and *Philadelphia* (1993), about discrimination against an AIDS victim.

His soft voice cracking with emotion, Reeve then told the actors, producers, and directors in the audience,

> When I was a kid, my friends and I went to the movies just for fun. But then we saw [director Stanley] Kubrick's *Dr. Strangelove*—it started us thinking about the madness of nuclear destruction. Stanley Kramer's *The Defiant Ones* taught us about race relations. And we began to realize that films could deal with social issues.
>
> Let's continue to take risks, let's tackle these [controversial and social relevance] issues many ways. The film community can do it better than anyone else. There is no challenge artistic or otherwise that we can't meet. Thank you.

At the Academy Awards ceremonies in 1996, Reeve appeals to the entertainment industry to put social causes ahead of profits.

Surprising even himself, Reeve returned to sailing that July. In his wheelchair strapped to the boat, he and Dana joined a crew aboard a sailboat in a race off Newport, Rhode Island. The race was held as a fund-raiser for Shake-A-Leg, a national non-profit organization providing posttraumatic rehabilitation for those with SCI and other neurological disorders.

Reeve was particularly gratified at becoming host of the 1996 Paralympics opening ceremony in Atlanta, Georgia, that August. Those in attendance numbered sixty-four thousand including paralysis victims and their families. "To be surrounded by people who believe in you is one of life's most precious gifts," he said to those paralyzed. "Look around you, and see how many people believe in you."[93]

Following the Paralympics, Reeve kept moving. He received the National Courage Award from the Courage Center in Minneapolis, at that rehabilitation center's Celebration of Courage ceremony in October. As he accepted the award, he spoke again in support of more federal funding to aid the disabled with their finances and for research to find cures for paralysis victims.

His next appearance was at the opening of the National Horse Show in New York's Madison Square Garden. There, equestrians saluted him at the event, which was dedicated to benefit the Reeve-Irvine Research Center; he asked Dana, who was at his side, to return the salute for him.

Still a horse enthusiast, Reeve attends the National Horse Show in Madison Square Garden. Dana is next to him on the left.

Reeve continued his twin campaigns for spinal cord research and increased insurance caps in 1997. He lobbied congressional legislators that even $100 million in additional research funds would be cost-effective because that is less than is being spent each year to merely maintain health care for injured citizens.

In June, Reeve testified before a Senate subcommittee that medical researchers are close to discovering how to regenerate damaged nerves in the spinal cord. He went on to plead for funds to continue that work. "Nearly a quarter-million Americans live with varying degrees of incapacity due to spinal cord injuries," he said. "How do we stop the economic and human cost of these diseases? The answer is research."[94]

The year was to end on a positive note for spinal cord research. That November, Reeve announced on the ABC television show, "The View," that he had gotten an e-mail from one of the world's top spinal cord injury researchers, Dr. Wise Young of New York University Medical Center, on latest attempts in spinal cord regeneration.

With Dana by his side, Reeve testifies at a Senate subcommittee hearing in 1997 in favor of increasing funding for medical research.

Democratic National Convention Speech

Reeve was a sensation when he spoke from his wheelchair on August 26, 1996, at the Democratic Party's national convention in Chicago. After receiving a tumultuous ovation when he was wheeled onto the convention stage, he got another a few minutes later when he told the thousands there and on television,

> The last few years we've heard a lot about something called family values. And like many of you, I've struggled to figure out what that means. Since my accident, I found a definition that seems to make sense. I think it means that we're all family. And we all have value.

Again the thousands of convention delegates rose to their feet and applauded, before Reeve continued,

> Now, if that's true, if America really is a family, then we have to recognize that many members of our family are hurting. . . . One in five of us have some kind of disability. You may have Parkinson's disease or a neighbor with a spinal cord injury or a brother with AIDS. And if we're really committed to this idea of family, we've got to do something about it.

> In my room when I was in rehab, there was a picture of the space shuttle blasting off. It was autographed by every astronaut down at NASA. On top of that picture it says, "We found nothing is impossible."

> Now, that should be our motto. It's not a Democratic motto, not a Republican motto. It's an American motto. It's not something one party can do alone. It's something we as a nation have to do together.

> If we can conquer outer space, we should be able to conquer inner space, too. And that's the frontier of the brain, the central nervous system and all the afflictions of the body that destroys so many lives and robs our country of so much potential.

"I can confidently tell you we will be able to have a cure within the seven-year period that you talked about," Reeve quoted Dr. Young. "The breakthrough has been the discovery of the antibody that knocks out the protein that prevents regeneration. Scientists now know what to do, they just need the dollars to go ahead and do it."[95]

The year 1998 was another busy one for Reeve as he continued his activism on behalf of paralysis victims. One highlight of the year was the nationally televised special, "Christopher

Reeve: A Celebration of Hope," in March. Robin Williams served as master of ceremonies for the event, which featured many guest celebrities, including Stevie Wonder, Mary Chapin Carpenter, Willie Nelson, Jane Seymour, Ted Danson, and Glenn Close. Dana Reeve wheeled her husband onstage for a speech in which he repeated his plea for funding for spinal cord research and assistance for the disabled.

As the 1998 Christmas shopping season approached, Reeve showed that he would do just about anything to raise money for spinal cord research. The Reeves appeared at a JC Penney department store in the Bronx, New York, to launch a new line of men's neckties designed by Dana and by movie stars Paul Newman, Glenn Close, and Ted Danson. Four percent of the sales of the ties, store officials announced, would be donated to the Christopher Reeve Foundation to aid spinal cord victims.

As 1999 opened, Reeve showed no signs of slowing down. In fact, he had increased his public appearances to twenty a year. As of early 1999, he had raised $2 million for the American Paralysis Association and the Christopher Reeve Foundation.

Chapter 7

Beyond Activism

During three years of undergoing extensive and often painful rehabilitation, including daily physical therapy sessions, Christopher Reeve not only found time for medical and political activism, he produced a best-selling book about his life. He also resumed his acting career and added something new to his credits, becoming a highly respected director.

A Quadriplegic Family

Dana Reeve told a reporter what her husband's life is like as he waits for a cure for spinal cord injury: "Chris is incredibly resilient. He will occasionally get down, hit rock bottom. I just listen, and try to find things that can help. Close physical contact is helpful. We decided I must be his wife, and not his nurse."[96]

Early in his rehabilitation, Reeve insisted that his disability should not prevent his wife from resuming her career. Dana Reeve began to appear in plays, both in summer theaters and on Broadway. Reeve was in the audience when she appeared in Clifford Odets's drama *The Big Knife* at his beloved Williamstown Theater Festival on June 22, 1998. That fall, she starred on Broadway in the comedy, *More to Love: A Big Fat Comedy*, playing the wife of an overweight comic.

Dana also told another reporter that she is hopeful about her husband's recovery. "Ten years ago the thinking was spinal cords do not regenerate. Five years ago scientists were hopeful they could do something. Today they expect they will.

"If something good has come out of this, it's that Chris's celebrity has educated people to the plight of so many people who got injured but who can still lead active, strong lives."[97]

Superman Really Matters

Reeve told an interviewer for the March 14, 1988, issue of *Time* magazine that he was inspired by meeting many disabled people after he made the Superman movies:

> I've seen first-hand how Superman actually transforms people's lives. I have seen children dying of brain tumors who wanted as their last request to be able to talk to me, and have gone to their graves with a peace brought on by knowing that their belief in this kind of character is intact.
>
> I've seen that Superman really matters. They're connecting with something very basic: the ability to overcome obstacles, the ability to persevere, the ability to understand difficulty and to turn your back on it.

She said their son, Will, helps a lot. They play hockey with Reeve driving his wheelchair in a zigzag and pretending to smooth out the ice. They also play board games, but Will has to roll the dice. However, Reeve admits he misses the times before his accident, when he played the piano with Will sitting on his lap and they would sing together.

In a January 1999 radio interview, Reeve spoke of how important his wife and three children are to him and added, "I don't want other people to be dragged down by the fact that I had a silly accident. So I try as hard as possible, and this is the most important lesson I've learned since the accident, and something I would pass on to other disabled people, and that is, even when you're feeling needy, your job is to give."[98]

Reeve elaborated on giving of himself to others in another interview, saying it is vital that he not lean too hard on his friends, wife, or children. "There are times I need something, or to be consoled. But I have to give instead of taking, so I can set people free. I have to make sure my children can go off to school without worrying about me."[99]

Reeve Returns to Work

Reeve knew that his role as an activist, while satisfying, could not fulfill all his needs. By the spring of 1996, he could breathe for half an hour without using a ventilator. Needing not only money to pay for his medical bills that were far beyond his insurance coverage, but to satisfy at least part of his hunger to perform again, he found some work he could manage. He narrated the role of the hero in a CD-ROM adventure game titled *9.* He was also signed to speak the voice of King Arthur for an animated movie, *The Quest for Camelot,* but was disappointed when, because of scheduling conflicts, the role went instead to actor Pierce Brosnan.

Uncertain if he could ever return to acting, Reeve took on another challenge in 1997 by directing an HBO made-for-television movie. *In the Gloaming,* starring Glenn Close and Robert Sean Leonard, was about a young man dying of AIDS.

Reeve was very gratified by the critical response to the movie. "It got respectable ratings, but the reviews were extraordinary," Reeve said in *Still Me.*[100]

In the Gloaming became 1997's most-honored single program at the 19th annual CableACE television awards, including being named as best dramatic or theatrical special.

Reeve directs Robert Sean Leonard in the HBO production of In the Gloaming.

Fellow activist and film star Glenn Close poses with Reeve at the premiere of In the Gloaming *in April 1997 in Los Angeles.*

Reeve's direction won him a Christopher Award from the Christophers, a national Catholic organization that each year honors work in film, television, and books "that expresses the highest values of the human spirit."

Reeve's Autobiography Is Published

Reeve then wrote a book about his life both before and after his accident, dictating it to an assistant, June Fox. He titled it *Still Me,* recalling his wife's words to him shortly after his accident: "You are still you, and I love you."[101]

"There's a double meaning to the word 'still,'" he told Larry King on television after the book was published in 1998. "I am still me, I continue to be me. And also, the fact that I don't move. So it's both. It was my title."[102]

Reeve told King that writing the book "was both therapeutic and emotionally difficult. I had to be matter-of-fact, not self-pitying."[103]

Reeve said he could not just give up after becoming paralyzed. "There are really only two choices, either you just stare out the window and do nothing, or you try to motivate and activate. That's the only way I could go." [104]

Many publications ran interviews with Reeve about his book and he also promoted it on television talk shows, including those hosted by Oprah Winfrey, Barbara Walters, and Larry King. Book reviewers gave *Still Me* high critical praise, and it quickly became a best-seller.

Reeve also made an audiotape recording of the book. In its introduction he says, "The audio book allows me to communicate with you in a very personal way, second only to being in the same room. I am very grateful for the power of the spoken word." [105] The audio book won him a Grammy award from the recording industry in the category of best spoken-word album.

A Triumphant Return to Acting

Following the huge success of his book, Reeve further challenged himself by doing what some had thought would be impossible. He made a comeback as an actor. The perfect role for that, he decided, would be in a remake of the classic 1954 Alfred Hitchcock thriller, *Rear Window*, because the lead character was confined to a wheelchair.

Reeve Is Lauded for *Still Me*

Typical of critics' praise for *Still Me* was Lisa Schwartzbaum's review in the May 8, 1998, edition of *Entertainment Weekly*:

Reeve's autobiography is distinguished not only by the dignified candor with which he describes his utterly changed world—that of a rich and famous movie star whose affluence and celebrity cannot buy the ability to hug his wife and three children—but also by his emotional directness.

Long hours of soul-searching have resulted in a heightened eloquence. Reeve communicates so well, in fact, that it's easy to forget that every word of *Still Me* has been wrested from a body in revolt against a mind clarified by adversity. This is a feat to daunt even Superman.

Reeve not only starred in the made-for-television movie that aired on Sunday night, November 22, 1998, on the ABC network, but was an executive producer. He also contributed to much of the script, changing the lead character he would play from a photographer with a broken leg to a quadriplegic, like himself.

"The reason I wanted to do this project," he said in a *TV Guide* interview, "was to play a seriously disabled person who, using his wits and assistive technology, is the film's hero."[106]

"What I wanted to show," he elaborated to another reporter, "was that you can get on with your life. It changes drastically, of course, but sometimes it brings new opportunities. I'm now president of a club [the severely disabled community] I wouldn't have wanted to join, and although I don't have as much of what I thought of as fun in the old days, I have some satisfaction which is deeper and more profound."[107]

Reeve recreates Jimmy Stewart's 1954 role as a disabled photographer who witnesses a murder in Rear Window.

Reeve was confident he was physically up to the acting job, which would require more than eleven hours a day for four weeks and would involve him in every scene. He said returning to acting was "just like getting on a bicycle. No problem."[108]

The physical effort required to make the movie seemed to reinvigorate Reeve. "Resting doesn't agree with me," he told Peter White in a British Broadcasting Company (BBC) radio interview. "During *Rear Window*, I had unlimited energy. I was in the [wheel]chair for 15 hours a day for more than a month."[109]

"He willed himself through it," said Steven Haft, another executive producer on *Rear Window*. "After the final shot, he collected the crew and said no matter what happened to him the next day, he had made it through. You could read on his face the pride and relief."[110]

Besides impressing the television crew on the film, Reeve made an impact on his costar, Daryl Hannah: "He's a committed and serious actor, but he's really funny, too. There's so much life in him."[111]

Critical response was equally positive. Robert Bianco wrote about Reeve and the movie in *USA Today:* "Considering all he's had to overcome, merely getting through it has to be counted as a personal victory. That triumph alone, however, is not enough— not for an actor and not for an audience. More importantly for all, *Window* is an artistic victory as well. Reeve has learned to use what he still has to great effect, and he turns in a fine, sometimes deeply affecting, performance."[112]

Reeve's performance in *Rear Window* won him a Golden Globe nomination from the Hollywood Foreign Press Association for best actor in a movie made for television. He did not win that award, but he did win the 1999 Screen Actors Guild Award for outstanding performance by a male actor in a television movie or miniseries.

Preparing for Recovery

Reeve continued physical therapy in 1999 to regain movement and feeling and to keep his body in shape while he awaits a cure. He was able to breathe without his ventilator at least thirty

Reeve and Dana in a celebratory mood at the Golden Globe award ceremonies in January 1999.

minutes daily and, with the aid of high-tech exercise equipment, rode a stationary bicycle and even walked on a treadmill.

He stressed the importance of exercise to other paralysis victims in an interview for *WE,* a magazine for those with disabilities:

> If you let your muscles atrophy, if your bone density lessens, if your cardiovascular system is not exercised, it

will be much harder to benefit when new therapies come along. The scientist's job is to figure out how to deliver, and the patient's job must be physical readiness.[113]

"I'm the healthiest I've been since the accident, and I'm grateful," Reeve told a *Life* magazine reporter late in 1998, "because recovery will go to the fittest."[114]

Reeve and his wife were encouraged by the life he increasingly felt in his body, such as a sensation of pain when someone touched his spine.

Reeve's nurses said one of the best things he has going for him toward recovery is that he is highly motivated to get well again. Reeve agrees: "The mind plays a tremendous role in healing," Reeve has said. "It's not going to cause the nervous system to regenerate, but to cure a wound, breathe longer off the 'vent' or sit in a wheelchair and make a movie, you can control those kinds of things."[115]

Reeve is encouraged by research into spinal cord regeneration using antibodies and nerve growth factors. "I think human trials are a year away," he said in a 1998 interview. "There is only a 20-millimeter gap in my case," referring to the break in his spinal cord, "less than an eighth of an inch"[116] between paralysis and walking, moving his hands, breathing on his own.

The ultimate challenge for scientists is inducing damaged nerves to reconnect, forming networks that carry sensations of pain and pleasure, that lift a finger and propel a leg.

"For a hundred years the dogma was that the adult nervous system does not regenerate," said Dr. Fred Gage, a neuroscientist with the Salk Institute for Biological Studies, in 1996. "But now we know that is not true."[117] In one approach, researchers have tried grafting fetal nerve cells into the site of a nerve injury.

Gage was even more confident in an interview two years later. "There has been tremendous progress in the regeneration of the spinal cord. I am confident that in his lifetime Chris will be exposed to treatment that will have some significant effect on the quality of his life."[118]

Meanwhile, Reeve fans all over the world keep informed about his health and progress in spinal cord research as well as his career by logging onto the Christopher Reeve Homepage on the Internet: www.geocities.com/Hollywood/Studio/4071/.

Reeve Looks Ahead

Reeve's plans for the immediate future were to direct his wife in a movie adaptation of *Good Will*, an off-Broadway play Dana had starred in in the spring of 1998. Based on a novella by Pulitzer Prize–winning author Jane Smiley, it is about a family that moves to a farm to simplify their life.

Reeve has said he would love to do more acting, but roles for quadriplegics are rare. However, he has been sent many movie scripts and plans to continue directing.

"I'd love to see more films with a disabled person at the center of it, and for it not to be a big deal," he told one reporter. "It's just part of the American scene that there are 50 million people with disabilities, one-fifth of our population, and they should be seen more on the screen."[119]

To Christopher Reeve, the future looks bright. As he told an interviewer after filming *Rear Window* in 1998,

> I've pretty much beaten depression because I'm realistically able to look forward to a future that means recovering a normal life. In ten years I hope this all will be a bad dream.

The Busy Reeves

As Reeve progresses toward his recovery, his family goes on with their lives.

Of his children with Gae Exton, both are in England with their mother. Their son, Matthew Reeve, nineteen years old in 1999, is attending college. Their daughter, Alexandra, is in high school in England and working as a model, having appeared in a six-page spread in the January issue of a British magazine called *Tatler*.

Reeve's son with Dana, Will, is seven years old and attends public school.

Dana was continuing her acting career and completed work on a book called *Care Packages: Letters to Christopher Reeve*, which contains letters from people all over the world who wrote to the actor while he was in rehabilitation after his accident.

There are times when I indulge myself for a little while. First thing in the morning, I'll remember a trip to Maine or something that Dana and I did that was really special.

But I find that I cherish these things rather than resent that I can't do them anymore. I'm lucky that I had an exciting and adventurous life for 42 years. I have those memories and a realistic prospect of a better future. I don't have a legitimate cause to get down. I'm too busy to feel sorry for myself.[120]

Failure Is Not an Option

Christopher Reeve also continued his challenge to scientists to find a cure for spinal cord injuries. As he wrote in *Still Me*, "In 1961, President [John F.] Kennedy issued the challenge to land a man on the moon before the end of the decade. At the time, scientists thought the goal was impossible . . . but in July 1969 Neil Armstrong took that giant step for mankind."[121]

In his *WE* magazine interview for paralysis victims, Reeve said, "I . . . propose a similar challenge to medical science. This time the mission would be the conquest of inner space, the brain and central nervous system."[122] Reeve elaborated on this in *Still Me*, after President Clinton said on January 3, 1998, that his administration proposed to increase federal funding for the National Institutes of Health by $1 billion per year over the next five years, to provide for more medical research:

[President Bill Clinton] said that this century had been devoted to discoveries and achievements in the world around us, including the conquest of outer space. In the next century we should focus on solving the mysteries and conquering the difficulties of the world within us.

If the President and Congress follow through with the vision made public at the beginning of the new year [1999], it will be a major victory for all the advocates of research who have worked so long and hard to make this happen. I felt that a part of the speech I gave at the Democratic Convention [in 1996] had been validated: at

first something seems impossible; then it becomes im-
probable; but with enough conviction and support, it finally becomes inevitable. [123]

As he continues toward his goal to walk again, Reeve keeps in
mind the all-out effort to bring home the astronauts on the *Apollo
13* space mission in 1970. Determined to find a way to save the astronauts' lives, flight director Eugene Kranz at NASA had declared to the mission's ground crew, "Failure is not an option!" [124]
Reeve points in particular to the ingenuity the mission's team
showed in finding a way to bring the astronauts safely back to
earth when a carbon monoxide buildup inside their command
module gave them only thirty minutes to live.

"They improvised a solution," Reeve recalled in *Still Me.*
"Instructions were relayed to the spacecraft, and the astronauts
survived. To create an urgency [to find a cure for paralysis], and
to give the quest a human face, I declare my intention to walk

*Reeve endorses legislation that would create a national registry of those
with brain and spinal cord injuries, which would allow doctors to match
patients with the vital services they need.*

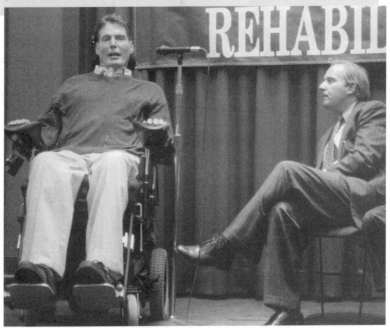

by my fiftieth birthday. The hope for speedy progress in the search for a cure for paralysis lies in the pooling of scientific information and financial resources." [125]

Some medical researchers see reasons for that hope. Dr. Wise Young, head of Rutgers University's Spinal Cord Injury [research] Project said in 1999 that almost all scientists believe that the spinal cord can be regenerated.

While he waits for that to happen, Reeve is making progress toward a recovery. He practices breathing without a ventilator for half an hour several times a day, and has gradually regained sensation in parts of his body, notably down the spine, in his left leg, and areas of the left arm. He is unable to move any part of his body below the shoulders, but continues his exercise daily so he is as physically fit as he can be for the day when a cure is found to spinal cord injury.

For Christopher Reeve, failure in his goal to walk again is not an option.

Notes

Chapter 1: A Boy in Search of a Family

1. Quoted in Adrian Havill, *Man of Steel: The Career and Courage of Christopher Reeve.* New York: Signet, 1996, p. 39.
2. Christopher Reeve, *Still Me.* New York: Random House, 1998, p. 60.
3. Quoted in Havill, *Man of Steel,* p. 41.
4. Reeve, *Still Me,* p. 60.
5. Quoted in Havill, *Man of Steel,* p. 40.
6. Reeve, *Still Me,* p. 74.
7. Reeve, *Still Me,* p. 79.
8. Reeve, *Still Me,* p. 79.
9. Reeve, *Still Me,* pp. 67–68.
10. Quoted in *Inside the Actors Studio,* television interview with James Lipton, Bravo Cable Channel, February 26, 1997.
11. Reeve, *Still Me,* p. 70.
12. Reeve, *Still Me,* pp. 70–71.
13. Reeve, *Still Me,* p. 71.

Chapter 2: From Apprentice Actor to Superman

14. Reeve, *Still Me,* p. 148.
15. Reeve, *Still Me,* p. 147.
16. Quoted in Havill, *Man of Steel,* p. 42.
17. Quoted in Libby Hughes, *Christopher Reeve.* Parsippany, NJ: Dillon Press, 1998, p. 27.
18. Quoted in Havill, *Man of Steel,* p. 48.
19. Reeve, *Still Me,* p. 51.
20. Quoted in Hughes, *Christopher Reeve,* pp. 30–31.
21. Quoted in Hughes, *Christopher Reeve,* p. 40.

22. Reeve, *Still Me,* p. 62.
23. Quoted in Havill, *Man of Steel,* pp. 48–49.
24. Reeve, *Still Me,* p. 165.
25. Reeve, *Still Me,* p. 167.
26. Quoted in Havill, *Man of Steel,* p. 51.
27. Quoted in Havill, *Man of Steel,* p. 53.
28. Quoted in *Inside the Actors Studio.*
29. Reeve, *Still Me,* p. 182.
30. Reeve, *Still Me,* p. 185.

Chapter 3: Fame and Personal Fortune

31. Quoted in *Inside the Actors Studio.*
32. Quoted in Lewis Archibald, "An Interview with Christopher Reeve: More than Meets the Eye," *Aquarian [NJ] Weekly,* April 7, 1982, p. 8.
33. Reeve, *Still Me,* p. 197.
34. Reeve, *Still Me,* p. 197.
35. Reeve, *Still Me,* p. 200.
36. Reeve, *Still Me,* p. 198.
37. Quoted in *Inside the Actors Studio.*
38. Quoted in *Inside the Actors Studio.*
39. Quoted in Havill, *Man of Steel,* p. 83.
40. Quoted in *Inside the Actors Studio.*
41. Reeve, *Still Me,* p. 203.
42. Quoted in Meredith Berkman, "Catching Up with Christopher Reeve: Up, Out, and Away," *Entertainment Weekly,* November 5, 1993, p. 43.
43. Reeve, *Still Me,* p. 203.
44. Reeve, *Still Me,* p. 201.
45. Reeve, *Still Me,* p. 202.
46. Reeve, *Still Me,* p. 183.
47. Quoted in Havill, *Man of Steel,* p. 161.
48. Reeve, *Still Me,* p. 82.
49. Quoted in Howard Kissel, "Wife Has Super Job," *New York Daily News,* March 16, 1998, p. 3.
50. Quoted in Havill, *Man of Steel,* p. 176.
51. Reeve, *Still Me,* pp. 80–81.
52. Quoted in *Inside the Actors Studio.*

Chapter 4: The Actor as Activist

53. Quoted in Havill, *Man of Steel,* p. 168.
54. Quoted in Havill, *Man of Steel,* p. 169.
55. Quoted in Havill, *Man of Steel,* pp. 169–70.
56. Reeve, *Still Me,* p. 228.
57. Quoted in Lou Cedrone, "Superman Relents: Reeve Takes on the Cape and Flies Once More," *Burlington County [NJ] Times,* July 23, 1987, p. 19.
58. "Gray Whales with Christopher Reeve," videotape recording. PBS Home Video, 1995.
59. Quoted in Elizabeth Mehren, "Reeve's Real-Life Human-Rights Role in Chile," *Los Angeles Times,* December 30, 1987, F1.
60. Quoted in Mehren, "Reeve's Real-Life Human-Rights Role in Chile."
61. Quoted in Mehren, "Reeve's Real-Life Human-Rights Role in Chile."
62. Quoted in Mehren, "Reeve's Real-Life Human-Rights Role in Chile."
63. Quoted in Mehren, "Reeve's Real-Life Human-Rights Role in Chile."
64. Quoted in Havill, *Man of Steel,* p. 189.
65. Quoted in Havill, *Man of Steel,* p. 189.
66. Quoted in Mehren, "Reeve's Real-Life Human-Rights Role in Chile."
67. Quoted in Hughes, *Christopher Reeve,* p. 63.
68. Quoted in Havill, *Man of Steel,* pp. 207–208.
69. Quoted in Havill, *Man of Steel,* p. 208.

Chapter 5: A Near-Fatal Accident

70. Quoted in Aljean Harmetz, "Somewhere in Time," *New York Times,* August 20, 1979, C13.
71. Reeve, *Still Me,* p. 19.
72. Quoted in Gregory Cerio, "Fallen Rider," *People Weekly,* June 12, 1995, p. 92.
73. Reeve, *Still Me,* p. 22.
74. Reeve, *Still Me,* p. 19.
75. Reeve, *Still Me,* p. 32.

76. Reeve, *Still Me,* p. 54.
77. Quoted in Barbara Walters, *20/20,* ABC television interview, September 29, 1995.
78. Quoted in Walters interview.
79. Reeve, *Still Me,* p. 37.
80. Reeve, *Still Me,* p. 37.
81. Reeve, *Still Me,* pp. 37–38.
82. Reeve, *Still Me,* p. 53.
83. Reeve, *Still Me,* p. 116.
84. Quoted in Christopher Reeve's speech at the 1996 Democratic National Convention, August 26, 1996. www.lib. uchicago.edu/~rd13/hd/reeve.html.
85. Quoted in Havill, *Man of Steel,* p. 236.
86. Quoted in Katie Couric, *Today Show,* NBC television interview, November 28 and 29, 1995.
87. Quoted in Havill, *Man of Steel,* p. 247.

Chapter 6: Activist in a Wheelchair

88. Quoted in David Frost, BBC radio interview, May 31, 1998.
89. Quoted in Larry King, *Larry King Live,* CNN television interview, May 5, 1998.
90. Quoted in Liz Smith, "We Draw Strength from Each Other," *Good Housekeeping,* June 1996, p. 172.
91. Quoted in Roger Rosenblatt, "New Hopes, New Dreams," *Time,* August 26, 1996, p. 42.
92. Quoted in Margaret L. Finn, *Christopher Reeve: Actor and Activist.* New York: Chelsea House, 1997, p. 114.
93. Christopher Reeve Homepage 1996, p. 4. www.geocities. com/Hollywood/Studio/4071/.
94. Christopher Reeve Homepage 1997, p. 2.
95. Christopher Reeve Homepage 1998, p. 5.

Chapter 7: Beyond Activism

96. Quoted in Dinitia Smith, "A Life with a Before and an After," *New York Times,* April 30, 1998, p. B4.
97. Quoted in Kissel, "Wife Has a Super Job," p. 3.
98. Quoted in Peter White, BBC radio interview, January 5, 1999.
99. Quoted in Jeffrey Zaslow, "The Uncommon Strength of Christopher Reeve," *USA Weekend,* May 15–17, 1998, p. 4.

100. Reeve, *Still Me,* p. 258.

101. Reeve, *Still Me,* p. 77.

102. Quoted in King, *Larry King Live.*

103. Quoted in King, *Larry King Live.*

104. Quoted in King, *Larry King Live.*

105. Reeve, *Still Me,* audio book introduction.

106. Quoted in Ileane Rudolph, "Christopher Reeve: Still Super," *TV Guide,* November 21–27, 1998, p. 27.

107. Quoted in Jefferson Graham, "Reeve's 'Window of Opportunity,'" *USA Today,* November 20, 1998, p. E11.

108. Quoted in Graham, "Reeve's 'Window of Opportunity.'"

109. Quoted in White, BBC radio interview.

110. Quoted in Rudolph, "Christopher Reeve: Still Super."

111. Quoted in Rudolph, "Christopher Reeve: Still Super."

112. Robert Bianco, "Reeve Delivers Intimate View of 'Rear Window,'" *USA Today,* November 20, 1998, p. E1.

113. Quoted in Todd Shapera, "The Real Window," *WE,* November/December 1998, p. 19.

114. *Life,* "A Life Redefined," November 1998, p. 68.

115. Quoted in Rudolph, "Christopher Reeve: Still Super."

116. Quoted in Smith, "A Life with a Before and an After."

117. Quoted in Kendall Hamilton, "Fighting to Fund an 'Absolute Necessity,'" *Newsweek,* July 1, 1996, p. 54.

118. Quoted in Rudolph, "Christopher Reeve: Still Super."

119. Quoted in Graham, "Reeve's 'Window of Opportunity.'"

120. Quoted in Rudolph, "Christopher Reeve: Still Super."

121. Reeve, *Still Me,* p. 134.

122. Quoted in Shapera, "The Real Window," p. 19.

123. Reeve, *Still Me,* p. 145.

124. Quoted in Reeve, *Still Me,* p. 135.

125. Reeve, *Still Me,* p. 135.

Important Dates in the Life of Christopher Reeve

1952

Christopher Reeve is born in New York City on September 25.

1956–59

Parents divorce in 1956; moves with mother and brother to Princeton, New Jersey; mother marries Tristam Johnson in 1959.

1962

Appears on stage in first play, singing in Gilbert and Sullivan's *The Yeoman of the Guard* at McCarter Theater, Princeton.

1968

Becomes apprentice actor at Williamstown Theater Festival in Williamstown, Massachusetts.

1970–74

Enters Cornell University in Ithaca, New York, 1970; attends Juilliard School of Drama in New York City in 1973; graduates from Cornell with B.A. in English and music theory in 1974.

1974–76

Plays Ben Harper on television soap opera *Love of Life*.

1975-76

Debuts on Broadway in *A Matter of Gravity* with Katharine Hepburn in 1975; makes movie debut in *Gray Lady Down* in 1976.

1977

Wins role of Superman.

1978
Begins living with British model Gae Exton.

1979
Son Matthew is born.

1983
Daughter Alexandra is born.

1986–1995
Engages in political, social, and environmental activism.

1992
Marries singer-actress Dana Morosini; they have son, William.

1995
Falls from horse in near-fatal horse-jumping competition in Virginia on May 27 and becomes a quadriplegic.

1995-1999
Resumes his television movie career while in paralysis rehabilitation and gains worldwide acclaim by becoming a wheelchair activist for spinal cord injury research and cure.

For Further Reading

Books

Judith Graham, ed., *Current Biography*. New York: Wilson, 1982. A biography of Christopher Reeve before his accident, summarizing his stage career and how and why he was chosen to play Superman in the movies.

Margaret L. Finn, *Christopher Reeve: Actor and Activist*. New York: Chelsea House, 1997. A biography of Christopher Reeve, appropriate for young adults. The author describes Reeve's life and career up to his accident in 1995 and the first two years of his rehabilitation and activism.

Libby Hughes, *Christopher Reeve*. Parsippany, NJ: Dillon Press, 1998. A biography of Christopher Reeve. Young adults can get an overview of Reeve's life and career in this short book for younger readers.

Works Consulted

Books

Adrian Havill, *Man of Steel: The Career and Courage of Christopher Reeve*. New York: Signet, 1996. This adult paperback biography of Christopher Reeve follows his life and career into the first year after his accident.

Christopher Reeve, *Still Me*. New York: Random House, 1998. Reeve's autobiography for adults. While Reeve's own account of his life and career is often engrossing, his style of switching back and forth from his accident and rehabilitation to other events in his life and career does not make it easy reading for young adults.

Periodicals

Lewis Archibald, "An Interview with Christopher Reeve: More than Meets the Eye," *Aquarian [NJ] Weekly*, April 7, 1982.

Meredith Berkman, "Catching Up with Christopher Reeve: Up, Out, and Away," *Entertainment Weekly*, November 5, 1993.

Robert Bianco, "Reeve Delivers Intimate View of 'Rear Window,'" *USA Today*, November 20, 1998.

Lou Cedrone, "Superman Relents: Reeve Takes on the Cape and Flies Once More," *Burlington County [NJ] Times*, July 23, 1987.

Gregory Cerio, "Fallen Rider," *People Weekly*, June 12, 1995.

Jefferson Graham, "Reeve's 'Window of Opportunity,'" *USA Today*, November 20, 1998.

Kendall Hamilton, "Fighting to Fund an 'Absolute Necessity,'" *Newsweek*, July 1, 1996.

Aljean Harmetz, "Somewhere in Time," *New York Times*, August 20, 1979.

Howard Kissel, "Wife Has Super Job," *New York Daily News*, March 16, 1998.

Connie Lauerman, "'Somewhere' Finds Its Time," *Chicago Tribune*, June 4, 1997.

Life, "A Life Redefined," November 1998.

Elizabeth Mehren, "Reeve's Real-Life Human-Rights Role in Chile," *Los Angeles Times*, December 30, 1987.

Roger Rosenblatt, "New Hopes, New Dreams," *Time*, August 26, 1996.

Ileane Rudolph, "Christopher Reeve: Still Super," *TV Guide*, November 21–27, 1998.

Lisa Schwartzbaum, "A Steely View," *Entertainment Weekly*, May 8, 1998.

Todd Shapera, "The Real Window," *WE*, November/December 1998.

Nancy Shute, "Reeve's Super Struggle," *U.S. News & World Report*, May 11, 1998.

Dinitia Smith, "A Life with a Before and an After," *New York Times*, April 30, 1998.

Liz Smith, "We Draw Strength from Each Other," *Good Housekeeping*, June 1996.

Robin Weiss, *Newsmakers '97*. Detroit: Gale, 1997.

Jeffrey Zaslow, "The Uncommon Strength of Christopher Reeve," *USA Weekend*, May 15–17, 1998.

Internet Sources

Christopher Reeve Homepage. Extensive information on Christopher Reeve's life and career, including summaries for the years 1996 to the present, and chat groups. www.geocities.com/Hollywood/Studio/4071/.

Christopher Reeve's speech at the 1996 Democratic National Convention, August 26, 1996. www.lib.uchicago.edu/~rd13/hd/reeve.html.

Radio

David Frost, BBC radio interview, May 31, 1998, in which Reeve tells how he copes with being a quadriplegic and of his hope to walk again.

Peter White, BBC radio interview, January 5, 1999, in which Reeve tells about his latest political activism and physical rehabilitation efforts.

Television and Video

Katie Couric, *Today Show,* NBC television interview, November 28 and 29, 1995. Reeve tells about his May accident and his life and health since then.

"Gray Whales with Christopher Reeve," videotape recording, PBS Home Video, 1995. Reeve narrates an hour-long color documentary for Meridien Productions on the life and habitat of endangered gray whales.

Larry King, *Larry King Live,* CNN television interview, May 5, 1998, in which Reeve relates highlights of his autobiography, *Still Me,* including his accident and subsequent medical treatment, resuming his career, and goals for the future.

James Lipton, *Inside the Actors Studio,* television interview for the Bravo Cable Channel, February 26, 1997. Reeve gives a lengthy, often funny, account of his life and career both before and after becoming a quadriplegic.

Barbara Walters, *20/20,* ABC television interview, September 29, 1995. Reeve is interviewed only a few months after his accident.

Index

Picture Credits

About the Author

Walter Oleksy writes novels and nonfiction books for preteens, young adults, and adults.

His novels include *If I'm Lost, How Come I Found You?; Bug Scanner and the Computer Mystery; Land of the Lost Dinosaurs;* and *The Pirates of Deadman's Cay.*

His nonfiction books include *The Information Revolution, Hispanic-American Scientists, The Philippines, Mikhail Gorbachev; A Leader for Soviet Change, The Black Plague,* and *Careers in the Animal Kingdom.*

Oleksy lives in a Chicago suburb with his dog Max, a black lab-shepherd mix who loves to swim and fetch tennis balls.